PLACE NAMES IN NEW YORK

07-GAZD

PLACE NAMES
IN NEW YORK

Why They Are So Called

Edward R. Gazda

07-GAZD

To order additional copies of this book, contact:
Xlibris Corporation
1-888-7-XLIBRIS
www.Xlibris.com
Orders@Xlibris.com

CONTENTS

DEDICATED TO MY BROTHER WILLIAM
WILLIAM "BILL" GAZDA
AND MY WIFE "EDNA" FOR HER PATIENCE

PREFACE

This booklet has been published to make it easier to access information regarding the source of the "Names of Places" in New York State.

The question "Why is it Named ?", asked over the course of many years, resulted in answers that comprise this booklet.

Reviewing the booklet will clearly confirm that "Place Names" in New York State have had contributions from the American Indians, the Dutch, the English, the French and the Scottish, in the state's early history and from through out the world there-after.

A good example is "New York" , which was named by the English to honor their Duke of York, after they defeated the Dutch for the New Amsterdam Colony, by combining the "New" from the old name with "York."

All names are listed in alphabetical order. In parenthesis following each county is the year in which the county was established and the county seat of each county. Following each community name, in parenthesis, is the name of the county in which it is located.

The sources of information are so many and so varied that it is impossible to acknowledge them all. The researcher acknowledges that all "Place Names" are not shown. It is also impossible to guarantee the correctness of all the information shown, but I believe it to be reliable.

JAN. 8, 20 01

NEW YORK STATE

Counties

1. **Albany (1683)** County seat, Albany. Named to honor the Duke of York, by his Scottish title, the Duke of Albany.

2. **Allegany (1806)** County Seat, Belmont. Named for the Allegany Indian tribe. The name means "people of the fine river", or the near-by Allegany River.

3. **Bronx (1914)** County seat Bronx. Name is the Anglicized name of Janas Bronck, early Dutch landowner. * Now a Borough of New York City.

4. **Broome (1806)** County Seat, Binghamton. Named for John Broome, statesman.

5. **Cattaraugus (!808)** County Seat, Little Valley. Named for the Cattaraugus Indian tribe. The name means "people of the bad smelling shore."

6. **Cayuga (1799)** County Seat, Auburn. Named for the Cayuga Indian tribe. The name means "people of the place were locust are taken out."

7. **Chautauqua (1808)** County seat, Mayville. Named for the Chautauqua Indian tribe. The name means "people of the foggy place."

8. **Chemung** (1798) County Seat, Elmira. Named for the Chemung Indian tribe. The name means "people of the big horn."

9. **Chenango** (1798) County Seat, Norwich. Named for the Chenango Indian tribe. The name means "people of the bull thistles."

P-130

10. **Clinton** (1788) County Seat, Plattsburgh. Named to honor George Clinton, Governor of New York State.

11. **Columbia** (1786) County Seat, Hudson. Named to honor Columbus, the Discoverer of America, using the Latin version of his name.

12. **Cortland** (1808) County Seat, Cortland. Name for Pierre Van Cortlandt, statesman.

P-102

13. **Delaware** (1997) County Seat, Delhi. Named for the Delaware Indian tribe or the Delaware River.

14. **Dutchess** (1683) County Seat, Poughkeepie. Named to honor Mary Beatrice d'Este, Dutchess of York, the wife of James, Duke of York, who became King James II of England.

15. **Erie** (1821) County Seat, Buffalo. Named for the Erie Indian tribe. The name is derived from an Indian word meaning" people of the panther."

16. **Essex** (1799) County Seat, Elizabethtown. Named after Essex County, in England.

17. **Franklin** (1808) County Seat, Malone. Named to honor Benjamin Franklin, statesman and Signer of the Declaration of Independence.

18. **Fulton** (1838) County Seat, Johnstown. Named for Robert Fulton, Governor of New York State.

19. **Genesee** (1802) County Seat, Batavia. Named for the Genesee Indian tribe, the name means "people of the beautiful valley."

20. **Greene** (1800) County Seat, Catskill. Named to honor General Nathaniel Greene, American Revolutionary War hero.

21. **Hamilton** (1816) County Seat, Lake Pleasant. Named to honor Alexander Hamilton, statesman and a leader In the American Revolution.

22. **Herkimer** (1791) County Seat, Herkimer. Named to honor General Nicholas Herkimer, American Revolutionary War hero.

23. **Jefferson** (1805) County Seat, Watertown. Named to honor President Thomas Jefferson, a Signer of the Declaration of Independence and a leader in the American Revolution.

24. **Kings** (1683) County Seat, Brooklyn. Named to honor King Charles II of England. * Now a Borough of New York City.

25. **Lewis** (1805) County Seat, Lowville. Named for Morgan Lewis, Governor of New York State.

26. **Livingston** (1821) County Seat, Genesco. Named to honor Robert Livingston, statesman.

27. **Madison** (1806) County Seat, Wampsville. Named to honor President James Madison.

28. **Monroe** (1821) County Seat, Rochester. Named to honor President James Monroe.

29. Montgomery (1772) County Seat, Fonda. Named to honor General Richard Montgomery, American Revolutionary War hero.

30. Nassau (1899) County Seat, Mineola. Named to honor William of Nassau, Prince of Orange, who became King William III of England.

31. New York (1683) County Seat, New York. Named to honor the Duke of York, who later became James II of England.

32. Niagara (1808) County Seat, Lockport. Named for the Niagara Indian tribe. The name means "people of the divided bottom land."

33. Oneida (1798) County Seat, Utica. Named for the Oneida Indian tribe. The name means "stone people."

34. Onondaga (1794) County Seat, Syracuse. Named for the Onondaga Indian tribe. The name means "people of the mountains."

35. Ontario (1789) County Seat, Canandaigua. Named for the Ontario Indian tribe. The name means "beautiful lake."

36. Orange (1683) County Seat, Goshen. Named to honor William Orange, Prince of Orange, who later became King William III of England.

37. Orleans (1824) County Seat, Albion. Named after Orleans, France.

38. Oswego (1816) County Seat, Oswego. Named the near-by Oswego River. The name means "the outpouring", referring to the mouth of the Oswego River.

39. Otsego (1791) County Seat, Cooperstown. Name is an Indian word meaning "place of the rock."

40. Putnam (1812) County Seat, Carmel. Named to honor General Israel Putnam, American Revolutionary War hero.

41. Queens (1683) County Seat, Jamaica. Named to honor "Queen" Catherine Broganza, wife of king Charles II of England. * Now a Borough of New York City.

42. Rensselaer (1791) County Seat, Troy. Named to honor Kiliaen Van Rensselaer, Dutch (landowner) Patroon.

43. Richmond (1683) (Staten Island) County Seat, St. George. Named to honor the Duke of Richmond, son of Charles II of England. * Now a Borough of New York City.

44. Rockland (1798) County Seat, New City. Name describes local "rocky" terrain.

45. Saint Lawrence (1802) County Seat, Canton. Named after the Saint Lawrence River, which was named by the French explorer, Jacques Cartier, who discovered the river.

46. Saratoga (1791) County Seat, Ballston Spa. Name is derived from an Indian word, meaning "place of swift water."

47. Schenectady (1809) County Seat, Schenectady. Name is derived from an Indian word, meaning "beyond the pine plains" or name derived from the Dutch term "schoon echten deel" meaning "beautiful, valuable portion of land."

48. Schoharie (1795) County Seat, Schoharie. Name is derived from an Indian word, meaning "driftwood."

49. Schuyler (1854) County Seat, Watkins Glen. Named to honor General Philip Schuyler, American Revolutionary War hero.

50. Seneca (1804) County Seat, Waterloo. Named for the Seneca Indian tribe name means "people of the stony area."

51. Steuben (1796) County Seat, Bath. Named to honor General Von Steuben, American Revolutionary War hero.

52. Suffolk (1683) County Seat, Riverhead. Named after Suffolk County, in England.

53. Sullivan (1809) County Seat, Monticello. Named to honor General John Sullivan, American Revolutionary War hero.

54. Tioga (1791) County Seat, Owego. Name is derived from an Indian word, meaning "between two points."

55. Tompkins (1817) County Seat, Ithaca. Named to honor Daniel Tompkins, Governor of New York State.

56. Ulster (1683) County Seat, Kingston. Named to honor the Duke of Ulster , brother of King Charles II of England.

57. Warren (1813) County Seat, Lake George. Named to honor Joseph Warren, statesman.

58. Washington (1772) County Seat, Hudson Falls. Named to honor President George Washington, a Signer of the Declaration of Independence and a leader of the American Revolution.

59. Wayne (1823) County Seat, Lyons. Named to honor General Anthony Wayne, American Revolutionary War hero.

60. **Westchester (1683)** County Seat, White Plains. Named after the city of Chester, England by early settlers, who utilized the fact, it was in a westerly location from England, resulted in the name "West"chester.

61. **Wyoming (1841)** County Seat, Warsaw. Named for the Wyoming Indian tribe. The name means "upon the great plain."

62. **Yates (1823)** County Seat, Penn Yan. Named to honor Joseph Yates, Governor of New York State.

CITIES, HAMLETS, TOWNS AND VILLAGES

Alberton (Nassau) Named for the founder Townsend Alberton.

Abbott (Cattaraugus) Named to honor Edward Abbott, Theologian.

Accord (Ulster) Name was chosen, to settle dispute or "accord" for a name for the town.

Acra (Greene) Name is derived from the Greek word "acral", which means extreme, possibly referring to the high elevation of the Village.

Adams (Jefferson) Named to honor President John Adams.

Adamsville (Rensselaer) Named for the founding Adams family and "ville" derived from the Latin word "villa" for village.

Addison (Steuben) Named to honor Joseph Addison, English statesman.

Adirondack (Warren) Named for near-by mountains and the Adirondack Indian tribe. The name means "bark eaters."

Adler Creek (Oneida) Name is derived from the German word "adeler" meaning eagle, that were once in abundance on the stream or "creek."

Adrian (Steuben) Named for a Roman Pope.

Afton (Chenango) Named after a stream in Scotland.

Akron (Niagara) Named after Akron, Ohio. The name is derived from Greek word meaning "summit."

Albany (Albany) Named to honor the Duke of Albany. Scottish title of the Duke of York, who became King James III of England.

Albertson (Nassau) Named for Townsend Albertson, early settler.

Albeyville (Lewis) Named for the founder, Henry Albey and "ville" derived from the Latin word "villa" for village.

Albion (Orleans) Name is a mythical name for England.

Alcove (Albany) Name describes the secluded location.

Alden (Erie) Named for the founding Alden family, early settlers.

Alexander (Livingston) Named for Alexander Rea, early settler.

Alexandria Bay (Saint Lawrence) Named for Alexander Leray, landowner using the Latin version of "Alexander" and the near-by "bay."

Alfred (Allegany) Named to honor King Alfred, of England.

Allegany (Cattaraugus) Name is derived from an Indian word meaning "fine river" or "long river."

Allentown (Allegany) Named to honor Ethen Allen, American Revolutionary War hero.

Alloway (Wayne) Name is derived from a Gaelic word meaning "rocky place."

Almond (Allegany) Name was chosen because "almonds" were abundant at the meeting, to name the town.

Alma (Allegany) Named after the city of Alma, Germany, by early German settlers.

Alplaus (Schenectady) Name is derived from a Dutch word meaning "place of eels", which were abundant in the near-by stream, during Colonial times.

Alpine (Schuyler) Named after the "Swiss Alps", by early Swiss settlers.

Altamont (Albany) Name is derived from a Latin word meaning "high mountain."

Altona (Clinton) Named after the city of Altona, Germany, by early German settlers.

Amagansett (Suffolk) Name is an Indian word meaning "place of good water."

Amawalk (Westchester) Name is an Indian word meaning "a gathering place."

Amber (Onondaga) Named after a river in England, name means "the river" in Gaelic.

Amboy Center (Oswego) Named after the city of Amboy, New Jersey and the fact that it was the local "center of commerce." Amboy is an Indian word meaning "hollow or valley."

Amenia (Dutchess) Name is derived from the Latin word "amoena"meaning "pleasant to the eye", by Amenia Society that founded the village.

Amenia Union (Dutchess) Named for the "union" of the town, which straddles the New York and Connecticut border and the Amenia Society that established the village.

Ames (Montgomery) Named for Fisher Ames, early settler.

Amherst (Erie) Named after the city of Amherst, Massachusetts, which was named to honor Sir Jeffrey Amherst, Colonial British military officer.

Amity (Allegany) Name is derived from the French word "amitie" meaning friendship. The name was chosen by the settlers to indicate that they were a friendly community.

Amityville (Suffolk) Named for the amicable settlement of an argument over what name the town should have.

Amsterdam (Montgomery) Named after the city of Amsterdam, in the Netherlands.

Ancram (Columbia) Named after Ancram in Scotland, ancestral home of the founding Livingston family.

Andes (Delaware) Named after the Andes Mountains in South America.

Andover (Allegany) Named after the city of Andover, Massachusetts.

Angelica (Allegany) Named to honor "Angelica" Schuyler Church, mother of the founder Philip Church.

Angola (Erie) Named for a former Kingdom in Africa.

Annandale on Hudson (Dutchess) Named after a local estate located on the shore of the Hudson River.

Annsville (Oneida) Named for the wife of the founder J. Bloomfield and "ville" derived from the Latin word "villa" for village.

Antwerp (Jefferson) Named after the city of Antwerp, Belgium, home of an early landowner.

Apalachin (Tioga) Name is a corruption of "Appalachian" the mountain system in which the village is located.

Apex (Delaware) Name describes the location at the top of a hill.

Appleton (Niagara) Named for the "Apple" Industry located there.

Apulia (Onondaga) Named after a district in Rome, Italy.

Aquebogue (Suffolk) Name derived from an Indian word meaning "land from the head of the bay."

Arcade (Wyoming) Named for a Roman architectural design. It was chosen by the residents because it was distinctive.

Ardsley (Westchester) Named after Ardley, England, reason for "s" is unknown.

Argusville (Schoharie) Named after "Argus" an Albany, New York newspaper. The name is derived from a Greek word meaning "ever watchful" and "ville" derived from the Latin word "villa" for village.

Argyle (Wyoming) Named after Argyleshire, Scotland, by early Scottish settlers.

Arietta (Hamilton) Named by Rensselaer Van Rensselaer, Patroon landowner to honor his mother.

Arkport (Allegany) Name is derived the fact that it once was a port used to harbor canal "Ark Boats."

Arkville (Ulster) Named for an incident, when after a flood the only building left standing was the home of "Noah Dimmick, thus the reference to the "Ark" and "ville" derived from the Latin word "villa" for village.

Arkwright (Cattaraugus) Named to honor Richard Arkwright, English statesman.

Arlington (Dutchess) Named to honor the Duke of Arlington.

Armonk (Westchester) Name is derived from an Indian word meaning "place of beaver."

Arthursburg (Dutchess) Named to honor president Chester Arthur and "burg" an English word meaning "town or borough."

Ashford (Cattaraugus) Named after Ashford Castle, in Ireland.

Ashland (Greene) Named after the home of Henry Clay, statesman.

Ashokan (Ulster) Name is derived from an Indian word meaning "small mouth or outlet."

Ashville (Chautauqua) Named for "Ash" trees once founded in the area and "ville" derived from the Latin word "villa' for village.

Assembly Point (Warren) Name is derived from an Indian word "Otyokwa" meaning "a gathering of people" or groups of Indians usually seen on this "point" of land.

Astoria (Queens) Named after John Jacob Astor, a famous resident.

Athens (Greene) Named after the city of Athens, Greece.

Athol (Warren) Named after the city of Athol, England.

Atlanta (Steuben) Named after the city of Atlanta, Georgia, name means "place of rest."

Atlantic Beach (Nassau) Name describes the "Beach" located on the Atlantic Ocean.

Attica (Wyoming) Named for a region near Attica, Greece, that looked similar to an early settler.

Attlebury (Dutchess) Named after Attleborough, England, reason for difference in spelling is unknown.

Auburn (Cayuga) Named for a locale in Oliver Goldsmith's poem "Desert Village."

Augusta (Oneida) Named after Augusta, Maine, by early settlers from there.

Aurelius (Cayuga) Named for Marcus Aurelius, Roman Emperor.

Auriesville (Montgomery) Named after a near-by stream, which was named for "Auries" or "Aaron's creek", for an early settler and "ville" derived from the Latin word "villa" for village.

Aurora (Cayuga) Name is derived from the Latin word meaning "Goddess of the Dawn."

Ausable Forks (Clinton) Name is derived from the French phrase meaning "at the sand."

Austerlitz (Columbia) Named to honor Napoleon's victory at the Battle of Austerlitz.

Ava (Oneida) Named after a City in Burma.

Averill Park (Rensselaer) Named for James Averill, landowner and the "park" like appearance of the area.

Avoca (Steuben) Name is claimed to be from Thomas Moore's "Sweet Vale of Avco."

Avon (Livingston) Named after an English River.

Babylon (Suffolk) Named after a biblical city in ancient Mesopotamia.

Bainbridge (Chenango) Named to honor William Bainbridge, American Revolutionary War hero.

Baiting Hollow (Suffolk) Named for the practice of early travelers, using the English word "baiting" or watering their horses in a local pond.

Balcom (Cattaraugus) Named for the founding Balcom family.

Baldwin (Nassau) Named to honor Francis Baldwin, statesman.

Baldwin (Chemung) Named for the founders Walter and Thomas Baldwin.

Baldwin (Nassau) Named to honor Francis P. Baldwin, statesman.

Baldwinsville (Onondaga) Named for the founder James Baldwin an "ville" derived from the Latin word "villa" for village.

Ballston (Saratoga) Named for Eliphalet "Ball", early settler "ton" is a contraction of "town."

Ballston Spa (Saratoga) Name is a contraction of Ballstown, named for Eliphalet Ball, early settler and the "health spa" once located there.

Balmat (Saint Lawrence) Named by early French settlers, to honor Jean de Balmat, who fought with Lafayette during the American Revolution.

Balmville (Orange) Named for large "palm tree" that once grew there and derived from the Latin word "villa" for village.

Bangall (Dutchess} Name is derived from Yankee phrase "well this does bang all" supposedly said when a horse was killed by a crowd in the Village.

Bangor (Franklin) Named after the city of Bangor, Maine, home of early settlers.

Barcelona (Chautauqua) Named after a city in Spain.

Barker (Broome) Named for John Barker, landowner.

Barkersville (Saratoga) Named for the Barker family, early settlers.

Barnerville (Schoharie) Named for Joseph Barner, early settler and "ville" derived from the Latin word "villa" for village.

Barrington (Yates) Named after the village of Barrington, Massachusetts, home of early settlers.

Barrytown (Dutchess) Named for the founding Barry family.

Barryville (Sullivan) Named to honor John Barry, statesman and "ville" derived from the Latin word "villa" for village.

Barton (Tioga) Named to honor Bruce Barton, statesman.

Batavia (Genesee) Named after the ancient Batavia, now a Province in the Netherlands.

Batchellerville (Onondaga) Named for the founding Batcheller family and "ville" derived from the Latin word "villa" for village.

Bath (Steuben) Named to honor Henrietta Laura, Countess of Bath, daughter of Sir William Pulteney, landowner.

Battenville (Wyoming) Name is derived from the abbreviation of Bartholomew Van Hogelboom, early settler on "Bart's kill" Dutch for stream or "Battenkill" and "ville" derived from the Latin word "villa" for village.

Bayport (Suffolk) Name describes the location of a "port" on the "bay."

Bay Shore (Suffolk) Name describes the location on "shore" on the "bay."

Bayville (Oneida) Name describes the location of a village on the bay and "ville" derived from the Latin word "villa" for village.

Beacon (Dutchess) Named for "fires" burned on near-by Mount Beacon as "warning beacons" during the Revolutionary War.

Bearsville (Ulster) Name Anglicized from Christian "Baehr", early settler and "ville" derived from the Latin word "villa" for village.

Beaverkill (Sullivan) Named for "beaver" located there, and the Dutch word "kill" meaning stream.

Beckers Corners (Albany) Named for Albertus Becker, early settler and the near-by highway intersection.

Bedford (Westchester) Named after the city of Bedford, England.

Beekman Corners (Schoharie) Named for the founder, William Beekman and the near-by highway intersection.

Belfast (Allegany) Named after Belfast, Ireland, by early Irish Settlers

Bellerose (Nassau) Name was chosen by the founder to give the community a distinctive name.

Belle Terre (Suffolk) Name is a French term meaning "beautiful earth" and was chosen by the founder, to make the name distinctive

Belgium (Onondaga) Named after the European nation, Belgium.

Bellmore (Nassau) Name was taken from the railroad station. The railroad chose the name to give the community a distinctive name.

Bellmont (Franklin) Named for the founder William Bell and the French word "mont" for mountain.

Bellport (Suffolk) Named for Thomas and John Bell, early settlers and the harbor or "port" located there.

Bellona (Yates) Named for Bellona, Roman Goddess of War.

Bellvale (Orange) Name is a combination of the French word "bell" meaning "beautiful" and the English word "vale" meaning low ground or shallow "valley" , to describe the valley as beautiful.

Belmont (Allegany) Named after the city of Belmont, Massachusetts, home of early settlers.

Belvidere (Allegany) Named after the city of Belvidere, Canada, by early settlers from there.

Bemis Heights (Saratoga) Named for John Bemis, early settler and the high ground on which it is located.

Bemis Point (Chautauqua) Named for the founding Bemis family and the "point" of land on which it is located.

Bennetsville (Broome) Named for the founding Bennett family and "ville" derived from the Latin word "villa" for village.

Bennington (Wyoming) Named after the city of Bennington, Vermont, by early settlers.

Benson Mines (Saint Lawrence) Named for the Benson family, mine owners.

Benton (Yates) Named for Levi Benton, early settler.

Benton Center (Yates) Named for Levi Benton, early settler and the commercial center located there.

Bergen (Genesee) Named after "Bergen-op-zoo" a city in the Netherlands.

Berkshire (Niagara) Named after the city of Berkshire, England.

Berlin (Rensselaer) Named after the city of Berlin, Germany, home of early settlers.

Berne (Albany) Named after the city of Berne, Switzerland, which was the birthplace of Jacob Wiedman, leader of the early Palatine settlers.

Bernhards Bay (Oswego) Named for the founding Bernhards family and the near- by bay.

Bethleheim (Albany) Named to honor the birthplace of the Christian Savior in Palestine, by early settlers.

Bethpage (Nassau) Named after the biblical village of Bethany.

Big Flats (Chemung) Name describes location on the "big flat area" on the banks of the Chemung River.

Big Indian (Ulster) Named for a legendary Indian named "Winnesook."

Big Moose (Herkimer) Named for the abundance of "Moose", once found in the area.

Billings (Dutchess) Named for the founder Josh Billings.

Billington Heights (Westchester) Named after the city of Billington, England and the location on high ground.

Binghamton (Broome) Named for the founder, William Bingham.

Birdsall (Allegany) Named for John Birdsall, early settler.

Bishopville (Allegany) Named for the founding Bishop family and "ville" derived from the Latin word "villa" for village.

Black Brook (Clinton) Named for the "brook's" dark or "black" color.

Black Creek (Allegany) Named for near-by "creek", which had a "dark color."

Black River (Jefferson) Named for near-by "river" which had a "dark color."

Blakeville (Erie) Named for the founding Blake family and "ville" derived from the Latin word "villa" for village.

Bleecker (Fulton) Named for Barent Bleecker, landowner.

Blenheim (Schoharie) Named for the "Blenheim" Land Patent, was named after the famous European Military Battle of Blenheim.

Bliss (Wyoming) Named to honor General Howard Bliss, American Revolutionary leader.

Blockville (Chautauqua) Named for the founding Block family and "ville" derived from the Latin word "villa" for village.

Bloomingdale (Essex) Named after the city of Bloemendan, in the Netherlands, the name means "Valley of flowers", which was Anglicized by English settlers.

Bloomfield (Onondaga) Named to honor Leonard Bloomfield, statesman.

Blooming Grove (Orange) Named for the good soil and fruit crops, that "bloomed" in the area, which made the town prosperous.

Blue Mountain Lake (Hamilton) Named for the"blue color" of the trees as seen at dawn or dusk.

Blue Point (Suffolk) Named for the famous "Blue Point" Oyster, that was once caught in abundance by the local baymen.

Blue Ridge (Essex) Name describes "bluish colored trees" on a near-by mountain "ridge."

Blue Stores (Columbia) Named for "blue colored store buildings", that were once located there.

Bluff Point (Yates) Name describes a "cliff" on a "point" of land that over looks Keuka Lake.

Boght Hills (Albany) Name is derived from Dutch word "boght" meaning "bend in the river", referring to the large bend in the near-by river and the hills located there.

Bohemia (Suffolk) Named for a former European Kingdom.

Boiceville (Ulster) Named for the founding Boice family and "ville" derived from the Latin word "villa" for village.

Bolivar (Allegany) Named to honor Simon Bolivar, South American patriot.

Bolton (Warren) Named after the city of Bolton, Massachusetts.

Bolton Landing (Warren) Named after Bolton Township and the village boat "landing."

Bombay (Franklin) Named for birthplace of Michael Hogan's wife, early landowner.

Boonville (Oneida) Named for Garrett Boon, agent for landowner, the Holland Land Company and "ville" derived from the Latin word "villa" for village.

Borodino (Onondaga) Named after a village in Russia.

Boston (Erie) Named after the city of Boston, Massachusetts, by early settlers who came from there.

Bouckville (Madison) Named for the founder John Bouck and "ville" derived from the Latin word "villa" for village.

Bovine (Dutchess) Named to honor the "cow" on which the local economy was based.

Bowmansville (Erie) Named to honor Isalah Bowman, statesman and "ville" derived from the Latin word "villa" for village.

Boylston (Rensselaer) Named for Thomas Boylston, landowner.

Bowerstown (Otsego) Named for the founding Bower family.

Bradford (Steuben) Named for William Bradford, landowner or after the city of Bradford, New Hampshire.

Braeside (Rensselaer) Name is derived from the Scottish word "brae" meaning "hill" and the word "side" meaning slope of a hill.

Braddack Heights (Monroe) Named to honor General Edward Braddack, military leader during the French and Indian Wars.

Bradford (Steuben) Named to honor General Bradford, Revolutionary War hero.

Brainard (Rensselaer) Named for David Brainard, early settler.

Brainardville (Franklin) Named for the founder Jeremiah Brainard and "ville" derived from the Latin word "villa" for village.

Braman Corners (Schenectady) Named for the founding Braman family, early setters and the near-by roadway intersection.

Branchport (Yates) Named for the "port's" location, on a "branch" of Keuka Lake.

Brant (Erie) Named for Indian Chief Joseph Brandt. The reason the "d" was eliminated is not known.

Brantingham (Lewis) Named for the founder Hopper Brantingham.

Briarcliff Manor (Westchester) Name describes location of a "manor" home on a "cliff" where "briars" shrubs grew.

Brasher Center (Saint Lawrence) Named for the founder, Philip Brasher and commercial center located there.

Brasher Falls (Saint Lawrence) Named for the founder, Philip Brasher and a near-by water falls.

Breakabeen (Schoharie) Name is derived from a German term meaning "Rushes that grew on the creek banks."

Brentwood (Suffolk) Named after the City of Brentwood, England.

Brewerton (Oswego) Named after Fort Brewerton, which was named to honor Captain David Brewerton, the first commander of the Fort.

Brewster (Putnam) Named for James and Walter Brewster, land-owners.

Briarcliff Manor (Westchester) Name describes location of the "manor" house on the high "cliff."

Brideville (Sullivan) Named for the "Bridge" and "ville" derived from the Latin word "villa" meaning village.

Bridgehampton (Suffolk) Named for the "bridge" that was built over a pond in the village and "Hampton" to conform with neighboring Hampton Villages.

Bridgewater (Oneida) Named to honor the Duke of Bridgewater.

Bridgewaters (Suffolk) Named for the artificial lakes in the area.

Brinckerhoff (Dutchess) Named for the founder, Derrick Brinckerhoff.

Bristol (Ontario) Named after the city of Bristol, Massachusetts.

Broardalbin (Fulton) Name is derived from "breadalbane", a district in Scotland.

Brockport (Monroe) Named for Neil Brockport, early settler.

Brocton (Chautauqua) Named after the city of Brocton, Massachusetts, by early settlers.

Brodhead (Ulster) Named for Charles Brodhead, landowner.

Broome (Schoharie) Named to honor John Broome, Lieutennant Governor of New York State.

Bronx (See Bronx County)

Bronxville (Bronx) Named after the "County or Borough" of the "Bronx" In which it is located, which was named for Janas Bronck, Dutch landowner and "ville" derived from the Latin word "villa" for village.

Brookburg (Ulster) Named for the founding Brook family and the English word "burg" for town.

Brookfield (Oneida) Named for the streams and fields of farmland, in the area.

Brookhaven (Suffolk) Named for the location on a "brook", which provided a safe "haven" for ships.

Brooklyn (Kings) Name is derived from a Dutch word "Breukelen", which means "broken land", referring to the rough and rocky terrain of the area in colonial times. it is a Borough of New York city.

Brooktondale (Tompkins) Named for founding Brookton family and "dale" or valley where it was located.

Brookview (Rensselaer) Named to describe the location overlooking the near-by "brook."

Brownville (Jefferson) Named to honor General Jacob Brown, hero of the War of 1812 and "ville" derived from the Latin word "villa" for village.

Brunswick (Rensselaer) Named to honor King George III of England who was from the German House of Brunswick.

Brutus (Cayuga) Named for "Brutus" Junius, a Roman statesman

Buchanan (Westchaster) Named to honor President, James Buchanan.

Buffalo (Erie) Name is derived from the French word "beaufleuve" meaning "beautiful river."

Bullville (Orange) Named for Thomas Bull, early settler and "ville" derived from the Latin word "villa" for village.

Burke (Franklin) Named to honor Edmund Burke, British Statesman

Burnwood (Columbia) Named for "fires" used to "burn wood" in the process of making charcoal.

Burt (Niagara) Named for "Burt" Van Horn, early settler.

Burtonville (Montgomery) Named for Judiah Burton, early settler and "ville" derived from the Latin word "villa" for village.

Bushnellville (Greene) Named for founder, Aaron Bushnell and "ville" derived from the Latin word "villa" for village.

Busti (Chautauqua) Named for Paul Busti, landowner.

Buskirk (Rensselaer) Named for Martin Van Buskirk, early settler.

Butler Center (Wayne) Named for founder, John Butler and that it was the local "center of commerce."

Butternut (Otsego) Named for the "Butternut" trees once located in the area.

Byron (Genesee) Named to honor Lord George Byron, English poet.

Cadiz (Cattaraugus) Named after the city of Cadiz, Spain.

Cadyville (Clinton) Named for Daniel Cady, landowner and "ville" derived from the Latin word "villa" for village.

Cairo (Greene) Named after the city of Cairo, Egypt.

Calcium (Jefferson) Named for the "Calcium" mined in the area.

Caledonia (Livingston) Name was the Roman name for Scotland.

Callicoon (Sullivan) Named for near-by stream, name derived from the Dutch word meaning"turkey."

Calverton (Suffolk) Named for Bernard Calvert, the hamlet's first postmaster the reason for the addition of "ton" is unknown.

Campbell Hall (Orange) Named for the founding Campbell's family home or "hall."

Cambria (Niagara) Name is derived from the Latin word for the"Wales" a district in England.

Cambridge (Washington) Named after the city of Cambridge, England.

Camden (Oneida) Named after the city of Camden, New Jersey, which was named to honor Sir Charles Pratt, Earl of "Camden."

Cameron (Steuben) Named for the founder Dugald Cameron.

Camillus (Onondaga) Named for a Roman general.

Campbell (Steuben) Named for John Campbell, early settler

Camphill Village (Columbia) Named after an estate located in Aberdeen, Scotland.

Campville (Tioga) Named to honor the founder Colonel Asa Camp.

Canaan (Columbia) Named after Canaan, Connecticut, by early settlers from there.

Canadice (Yates) Name is derived from Indian word "shenadice" meaning "long lake."

Canajoharie (Montgomery) Name is derived from an Indian word meaning "pot that washes itself", referring to a large pothole at the entrance to the Canajoharie Gorge.

Canandaigua (Ontario) Named for an Indian village "kanandargue", name means "town set off or chosen spot."

Canastota (Madison) Name is derived from an Indian word "knistestota" meaning "still or motionless cluster of pine trees."

Caneadea (Allegany) Name is derived from an Indian word meaning "where the heavens rest on the earth."

Canisteo (Steuben) Name is derived from an Indian word "Kanesstie" meaning "head of water."

Canoga (Seneca) Name is derived from an Indian word meaning "Oil floating on the water."

Canton (Saint Lawrence) Named after Canton, a district in Switzerland, by early Swiss settlers or the city of Canton, China.

Cape Vincent (Jefferson) Named for Vincent Bonaparte, landowner and the near-by land jutting out into the Saint Lawrence River.

Cardiff (Onondaga) Named after the city of Cardiff, Wales.

Carlisle (Cortland) Named for Carisle Pierce, landowner.

Carmel (Putnam) Named for a biblical mountain.

Carroll (Chautauqua) Named for the founder Charles Carroll.

Carrolton (Cayuga) Named for G. Carrolton, landowner.

Carthage (Jefferson) Named after an ancient African city-state.

Cassadaga (Chautauqua) Name is derived from an Indian word meaning "under the rocks."

Castile (Wyoming) Named after the city of Castile, Spain, by early settlers.

Castleton on Hudson (Columbia) Named for an ancient Indian dwelling located on "castle" hill over looking the Hudson River and "ton" the contraction of town.

Castorland (Lewis) Name is derived from the Latin word "castor" meaning "beaver" and the large land area surrounding the village."

Catatonk (Tioga) Name is derived from an Indian word meaning "big stream."

Catlin (Chemung) Named to honor the artist, George Catlin.

Cato (Cayuga) Named for the Roman statesman, Marcus Cato.

Catskill (Greene) Name for Jacob "Cats", a Dutch statesman and the Dutch Word "kill" meaning stream or for Dutch term "katskill" referring to the area as a place inhabited by wildcats.

Cattaraugus (Cattaraugus) Named for the "Cattaraugus" Indian tribe, name means "people of the bad smelling shore".

Caugdenoy (Oswego) Name is derived from an Indian word meaning "a place for eels."

Cayuga (Cayuga) Named for the Cayuga Indian tribe. The name means "people of the place where locust are taken out."

Cayuta (Schuyler) Name is an Indian word meaning "Mosquito Lake."

Caywood (Seneca) Named for the founding Caywood family.

Cazenovia (Madison) Named for Theophilus de Cazenove, agent for the Holland Land Company, landowner. The reason for the change in spelling is unknown.

Cedar Hill (Albany) Named for "cedar" trees that grew on the "hill".

Cedarhurst (Nassau) Named for a "cedar" grove that once grew in the area and the English Word "hurst" meaning a grove of woods.

Cedarvale (Onondaga) Named for the "cedar" trees that grew in the "vale" or valley.

Celoron (Chautauqua) Named for the French explorer, Pierre Celoron.

Cementon (Greene) Named for cement plants located there.

Centereach (Suffolk) Named for the location in the middle or "center" of Long Island.

Center Moriches (Suffolk) Name is derived from an Indian word meaning unknown and the city's location on the south "center" shore of Long island.

Center Point (Jefferson) Name describes "center" or central location in county.

Centerville (Allegany) Named for the village's location in the "center" of the district and "ville" derived from the Latin word "villa" for village.

Central Islip (Suffolk) Named for the location between the cities of Islip and East Islip.

Central Square (Oswego) Name describes "central" location of the village in the county.

Central Valley (Orange) Named for location in a "Valley" in the center of the county.

Centre Island (Nassau) Name describes island's central location in the lake.

Ceres (Allegany) Named for the Greek God of Grain or from a Gaelic word meaning "black water."

Chadwicks (Oneida) Named after the city of Chadwicks, England.

Chaffee (Cattaraugus) Named to honor Jerome Chaffee, statesman

Chambers (Chemung) Named for the founding Chambers family.

Champion (Jefferson) Named to honor General Henry Champion, a military leader during the American Revolution.

Champlain (Clinton) Named to honor the French explorer, Samuel Champlain.

Chapin (Ontario) Named to honor General Israel Chapin, war hero.

Charleston (Montgomery) Named for Charles Van Epps, early settler.

Charlotte (Monroe) Named to honor Charlotte Augusta, daughter of King George IV of England.

Charlotte Center (Chautauqua) Named after the city of Charlotte, Vermont and that the town was the "center" of local commerce.

Charlotteville (Schoharie) Named to honor Queen Charlotte, wife of King George III of England.

Charlton (Saratoga) Named to honor Doctor Charlton, noted physician of the era.

Chase Mills (Saint Lawrence) Named for the Chase family, mill owners

Chasm Falls (Franklin) Name describes location of near-by"chasm and waterfall."

Chateaugay (Franklin) Name is derived from the French word "chateuaga" for a "Seigniory", a feudal estate in France, atributed to early French explorers.

Chatham (Columbia) Named to honor William Pitt, statesman and the Earl of "Chatham."

Chaumont (Jefferson) Named for the founder James Chaumont

Chautauqua (Chautauqua) Name is derived from an Indian word meaning "foggy place."

Chazy (Clinton) Named to honor Lieutenant de Chazy, French officer killed there during the French and Indian Wars.

Cheektowaga (Erie) Name is derived from an Indian word meaning "crabapple place."

Chelsea (Dutchess) Named for "Chelsea" Paper Mill, the town's early major industry.

Chemung (Chemung) Name is derived from an Indian word meaning "big horn."

Chenango Bridge (Chenango) Name is derived from an Indian word meaning "bull thistles" and the local "bridge."

Cheneys Point (Chautauqua) Named to honor Benjamin Cheney, town benefactor and the location on a point of land.

Cheningo (Cortland) Name is a variant of Chenango also meaning "bull thistles."

Chepatchet (Otsego) Name derived from an Indian word meaning "chief turning place."

Cherry Creek (Chautauqua) Named for near-by stream and wild cherries that grew in the area.

Cherry Grove (Suffolk) Named for "groves of cherry trees" that grew in the area.

Cherry Plain (Rensselaer) Named for the "flat land and the cherry trees" grown there.

Cherry Valley (Otsego) Named for the abundance of wild "cherry" trees that once grew in the "valley."

Cheshire (Ontario) Named for the town of Cheshire, in England.

Chester (Orange) Named after the city of Chester, England.

Chestnut Ridge (Rockland) Name describes"chestnut trees that grew on a near-by hillside."

Cheviot (Columbia) Name is derived from the Scottish word "Cheviot." The name for the hills between Scotland and England.

Chichester (Ulster) Named for Samuel Chichester, early settler.

Chili Center (Monroe) Name is old name for the country of Chile and that the town was the local center of commerce.

Chilson (Essex) Named for the founding Chilson family.

Chippewa Bay (Saint Lawrence) Named for the "Chippewa" Indian tribe and the near-by "bay" of water.

Chittenango (Madison) Name is derived from an Indian word meaning "where the waters divide."

Churchtown (Columbia) Named for the founder Frederick Church.

Churchville (Monroe) Named for Samuel Church, early settler and "ville" derived from the Latin word "villa" for village.

Churubusco (Clinton) Named for the American Victory in the Mexican War.

Cicero (Onondaga) Named for a Roman statesman.

Cincinnatus (Cortland) Named for Roman War hero.

Circleville (Orange) Named for being located halfway between or the center of a "circle" between the villages of Bloomingburgh and the former Scothtown and "ville" derived from the Latin word "villa" for village.

Clarkson (Monroe) Named for Matthew Clarkson, landowner.

Claryville (Ulster) Named for the founding Clary family and "ville", derived from the Latin word "villa" for village.

Clay (Onondaga) Named to honor Henry Clay, statesman.

Claverack (Columbia) Name is derived from a Dutch term "racken" meaning a clover reach or field of clover. the name is attributed to the Explorer, Henry Hudson when he viewed the area covered with "clover."

Clayton (Jefferson) Named to honor John Clayton, statesman.

Clerverdale (Warren) Name was chosen, when the residents decided to change the community's name, from a suggested book title "Clerverdale Mystery" because it sounded unique.

Cliff Haven (Clinton) Name describes lake side "cliff" which provided a safe "haven" for ships from storms.

Clifton (Saint Lawrence) Named for the "Clifton" Iron Company, which founded the town.

Clifton Springs (Ontario) Named for the "cliffs and springs" located in the area.

Climax (Greene) Name was chosen by town officials, because nearby hamlets were named Result and Surprise, and felt there should be a "Climax."

Clinton Corners (Dutchess) Named for the founding Clinton family and the roadway intersection located there.

Clintondale (Ulster) Named for the founding Clinton family and the English word "dale" for valley.

Clintonville (Clinton) Named to honor George Clinton, Governor of New York State. and "ville" derived from the Latin word "villa" for village.

Clockville (Madison) Named for John Klock, landowner. Name became Anglicized with time and "ville" derived from the Latin word "villa" for village.

Clove (Dutchess) Name is derived from the Dutch word meaning "a canyon or gorge."

Clove Valley (Dutchess) Name is derived from a Dutch word meaning" a canyon or gorge", leading into the "valley" where it is located.

Clymer (Chautauqua) Named to honor George Clymer, statesman

Cobleskill (Schoharie) Named for Jacabus Kobell, early Dutch settler, who built a mill on the stream. The name was Anglicized by English settlers.

Cochecton (Sullivan) Name is derived from an Indian word "Cushetunk." meaning "place of red stone hills."

Cohoes (Albany) Derived from several Indian words meaning "a canoe falling, or little hollows or cradle holes at the waterfalls."

Cohocton (Steuben) Name is an Indian word meaning "branches or log in the water."

Coila (Washington) Named after a town in Scotland, home of early settlers.

Colchester (Delaware) Named after the city of Colchester, Connecticut. home of early settlers.

Coldenham (Orange) Named for the founding Coldenham family.

Colesville (Broome) Named for the founder, Edward Cole and "ville" derived from the Latin word "villa" for village.

Collamer (Onondaga) Named to honor Jacob Collamer, statesman

Collins (Cattaraugus) Named for the founding Collins family.

Collins Corners (Montgomery) Named for Stephen Collins, landowner and location at the intersection of two highways.

Collinsville (Lewis) Named for Homer Collins, early settler and "ville" derived from the Latin word "villa" for village.

Colonie (Albany) Name is derived from original "Colony" of Renssaerlaerwyk, which was applied to the little settlement that remained outside Fort Orange, during the era of Dutch control, which is now the city of Albany.

Colton (Saint Lawrence) Named for Jesse Colton Higley, early settler.

Columbiaville (Columbia) Named to honor the explorer, Christopher Columbus, using the Latin version of his name and "ville" derived from the Latin word "villa" for village.

Commack (Suffolk) Name is derived from an Indian word meaning "beautiful place."

Comstock (Washington) Named for John Comstock, early settler

Conesus (Monroe) Name is derived from an Indian word meaning "place where berries are abundant."

Conatantia (Oswego) Named is derived from "Consanta" in Romania, reason for difference in spelling is unknown.

Conesus (Livingston) Name derived from an Indian word meaning "place where berries are abundant."

Conesville (Schoharie) Named to honor the Reverend Jonathan Cone, Religious Leader and "ville" derived from the Latin word "villa" for village.

Conewango (Cattaraugus) Name is derived from an Indian word "ganoungo" meaning rapid stream.

Coney Island (Kings) Name is derived from the Dutch term "Konijn Eiland" meaning "Rabbit Island", due to the numerous rabbits that inhabited the island during Colonial times.

Congers (Rockland) Named for Abraham Conger, landowner.

Conklin (Allegany) & (Broome) Named for the founder, John Conklin.

Conklinville (Saratoga) Named for the founder Gurdon Conklin and "ville" derived from the Latin word "villa" for village.

Conquest (Otsego) Name is for the victory or "conquest" by the town's people of the town of Cato, who were opposed to a division of the town.

Constable (Franklin) Named for the founding Constable family.

Constableville (Franklin) Named for the founder William Constable and "ville" derived from the Latin word "villa" for village.

Cooksburg (Albany) Named for the founder Thomas Cook, and the English word "burg" for town.

Cooks Falls (Columbia) Named for the founding Cook family and the near-by water falls.

Coopers Plains (Steuben) Named for the founding Cooper family and the "flat land" in the area.

Cooperstown (Otsego) Named for the founder William Cooper.

Coopersville (Clinton) Named for the founder Ebenezer Cooper and "ville" derived from the Latin word "villa" for village.

Copake (Columbia) Name is derived from an Indian word "achkookpaug" meaning "snake lake."

Copenhagen (Lewis) Named after the city of Copenhagen. The capital of Denmark.

Copiague (Suffolk) Name is an Indian word meaning "sheltered harbor."

Coram (Suffolk) Name is derived from an Indian word meaning "a passage between hills or a valley."

Corbett (Columbia) Named for the founding Corbett family.

Coreys (Franklin) Named for the founding Corey family.

Corfu (Genesee) Named after Corfu an island in the Ionian Sea, found off the west coast of Greece.

Corning (Steuben) Named for the founder Erastus Corning , who established the Corning Glass Works, which was the city's major industry.

Corinth (Warren) Named after the city of Corinth in Greece.

Cornwall (Orange) Named after the city of Cornwall, Connecticut, by early settlers, which was named after Cornwall, England.

Cornwallville (Greene) Named for the founder Daniel Cornwall and "ville" derived from the Latin word "villa" for village.

Cortland (Cortland) Named to honor Pierie Van Cortlandt, statesman. The name was Anglicized by eliminating the "t."

Cortlandt (Westchester) Named to honor Pierie Van Cortlandt, statesman.

Cossayuna (Washington) Name is derived from an Indian word meaning "lake at the pines."

Coventry (Delaware) Named after the city of Coventry, Connecticut, home of early settlers.

Coventryville (Delaware) Named after the city of Coventry, Connecticut, and "ville" derived from the Latin word "villa" for village, added to differentiate it from the town of Coventry.

Covigton (Cayuga) Named for the founder Leonard Covigton.

Cowlesville (Wyoming) Named for the Founding Cowles family and "ville" derived from the Latin word "villa" for village.

Coxsackie (Greene) Name is derived from an Indian word meaning "hoot of the owl."

Cragsmoore (Ulster) Name is derived from the English word "cragmoor" meaning "rocks in a marshy area."

Craigsville (Orange) Named for the founder Hector Craig and "ville" derived from the Latin word "villa" for village.

Cranberry Creek (Fulton) Named for "cranberries" that grew there and near-by stream or "creek."

Cranesville (Montgomery) Named for the founder, David Crane and "ville" derived from the Latin word "villa" for village.

Craryville (Columbia) Named for the Founding Crary family and "ville" derived from the Latin word "villa" for village.

Crescent (Saratoga) Named for "crescent" or the bend in the near-by Mohawk River.

Crittenden (Erie) Named for the founding Crittenden family.

Croghan (Lewis) Named to honor Colonel George Croghan, hero in The War of 1812.

Cropseyville (Rensselaer) Named for Valentine Cropsey, early settler and "ville" derived from the Latin word "villa" for village.

Croton on Hudson (Westchester) Named for an Indian chief and the location on the Hudson River.

Crown Point (Warren) Name Anglicized from the French name "point auchevolure" meaning "point of hair or scalp" referring to a massacre that occurred there or it is the corruption of Dutch term "cruin punt" meaning the summit point or "kroom punt" meaning "scalp point."

Crugers (Sullivan) Named for the the founder, John Cruger.

Cuba (Allegany) Named after the island nation of Cuba.

Cuddelbackville (Orange) Named for William Cuddelback, landowner and "ville" derived from the Latin word "villa" for village.

Cummings Hollow (Montgomery) Named for Benjamin Cummings, landowner and the valley or "hollow" it was located.

Curry (Ulster) Name is derived from the Gaelic word "currie" meaning boggy plain or flat land, change spelling occurred as time past.

Cutchogue (Suffolk) Name derived from an Indian word meaning "principal place."

Cutting (Chautauqua) Named to honor Reverend S.Cutting, Religious Leader.

Cuyler (Cortland) Named to honor John Cuyler, officer in the French Indian Wars.

Cuylerville (Livingston) Named for William Cuyler, early settler and "ville" derived from the Latin word "villa" for village.

Daarkill (Ulster) Name is a Dutch word which means "a stream that changes current direction", which occurred at the mouth of this stream.

Dairyland (Ulster) Name describes local "dairy" industry.

Damascus (Broome) Named after the city of Damascus, Syria.

Danby (Tompkins) Named after the city of Danby, England.

Dannemora (Clinton) Named after Dannamoria, Sweden, due to similar terrain at each place.

Dansville (Livingston) Named for Daniel "Dan's" Faulkner, early settler and "ville" derived from the Latin word "villa" for village.

Danube (Herkimer) Named after the Danube River in Europe.

Darien (Genesee) Named after the city of Darien, Connecticut, home of early settlers.

Davenport (Delaware) Named for John Davenport, early settler

Day (Montgomery) Named to honor Eliphaz Day, a prominent citizen.

Dayanville (Lewis) Named for the founder Jonathan Dayan and "ville" derived from the Latin word "villa" for village.

Dayton (Cattaraugus) Named for the founder Elisha Dayton.

Deansboro (Oneida) Named for the founder Thomas Dean and the English word "boro" for town.

Decater (Otsego) Named to honor Stephen Decater, hero of The War of 1812.

Deerland (Hamilton) Name derived from the Gaelic word "deer" meaning forest "land."

Deer Park (Suffolk) Named because an early settler enclosed fenced in a "park" like area, which contained a large number of "deer."

Deer River (Lewis) Named by an explorer, due to the large number of "deer" seen along the "river."

Deferiet (Jefferson) Named for Baroness Jenika Deferiet, landowner.

Defreestville (Rensselaer) Named for the Defreest family, early settlers and "ville" derived from the Latin word "villa" for village.

De Kalb (Saint Lawrence) Named for the founding De Kalb family.

Delancey (Delaware) Named for John Delancey, landowner.

Delanson (Schenectady) Name is derived by combining letters from the name of the "Delaware and Hudson" Railroads, for which it was a junction point.

Delevan (Cattaraugus) Named for Jack Delevan, landowner.

Delhi (Delaware) Named for being the home of Judge Foote, known as the "Great Mongul", since Delhi, India, was the capital city of the real Great Mogul.

Delmar (Albany) Named for the founding de La Mare family.

Denmark (Lewis) Named after the European country of Denmark, home of early settlers.

Denning (Ulster) Named for the founding Denning family.

Dennison (Herkimer) Named for the founder, J. Dennison.

Depauville (Jefferson) Named for Francis Depau, early settler and "ville" derived from the Latin word "villa" for village.

Depew (Erie) Named to honor Chauncey Depew, statesman.

Depeyster (Saint Lawrence) Named for the founder, Frederick Depeyster.

Deposit (Delaware) Named for being a place of "deposit" or a storage point for lumber.

Dering Harbor (Suffolk) Named for Thomas Dering, statesman and the picturesque "harbor" on which it is located.

Deruyter (Madison) Named for the founding Deruyter family.

Dewitt (Onondaga) Named for Moses Dewitt, statesman.

Dewittville (Chautauqua) Named for the founding Dewitt family and "ville" derived from the Latin word "villa" for village.

Dexter (Franklin) Named for Samuel Dexter, statesman.

Diamond Point (Broome) Named for the "diamond" like quartz found in the area.

Dickinson (Franklin) Named for the founder, Daniel Dickinson.

Dix Hills (Suffolk) Named for Dick Pechegan, nick named "dix", early settler and near-by "hills."

Dobbs Ferry (Westchester) Named for Jeremiah Dobbs, who established the original ferry boat service.

Dolgeville (Herkimer) Named for the founder, Alfred Dolge and "ville" derived from the Latin word "villa" for village.

Dorloo (Schoharie) Name is a corruption of the name "Dorlach", a town in Germany, home of early settlers.

Dormansville (Albany) Named for founder Daniel Dorman and "ville" derived from the Latin word "villa" for village.

Dover Plains (Dutchess) Named after the city of Dover, England and the "flat land" or "plains" on which it is located.

Downsville (Delaware) Named for Abel Downs, early settler and "ville" derived from the Latin word "villa" for village.

Dresden (Yates) Named after the city of Dresden, Germany.

Dry Brook (Ulster) Name describes the stream or "brook" as shallow and often without water or "dry."

Dryden (Tompkins) Named to honor John Dryden, English poet.

Duane (Franklin) Named for James Duane, landowner.

Duanesburg (Schenectady) Named for the founder James Duane and the English name "burg" for town.

Dundee (Yates) Named after the city of Dundee, Scotland or for an old hymn of the same name.

Dunkirk (Chautauqua) Named after the city of Dunkerque, France, Anglicized to the present spelling.

Dunnsville (Schenectady) Named for Christopher Dunn, land-owner and "ville" derived from the Latin word "villa" for village.

Dunsbach Ferry (Albany) Named for J. Dunsbach, first ferry boat owner.

Durham (Greene) Named after the city of Durham, Connecticut, by early settlers from there.

Durhamville (Madison) Named after the city of Durham, Connecticut and "ville" derived from the Latin word "villa" for village, added to distinguish it from Durham.

Eagle (Wyoming) Named for the "eagles" that were once prominent in the area.

Eagle Bay (Hamilton) Named for the "eagles" in the area of the near-by "bay."

Eagle Mills (Rensselaer) Named for the "Eagle Flour Mill" that was once town's main industry.

Earlton (Hamilton) Named changed from "Urlton" to "Earlton", to assist mail delivery, due to the misspelling of the prior name.

Earlville (Chenango) Named to honor John Earl, Canal Commissioner, when the canal was the Village's main industry and "ville" derived from the Latin word "villa" for village.

East Aurora (Erie) Named for the location "east" of the Hudson River and the Roman Goddess of Dawn.

East Branch (Delaware) Named for "east branch" of a near-by stream.

East Greenbush (Rensselaer) Name is derived from the Dutch term "grunen bosh" meaning "green woods", which was Anglicized to "Greenbush" and it's location east of the Hudson River.

East Marion (Suffolk) Named to honor General Francis Marion (Swamp Fox), military leader during the American Revolutionary War, the "east" was added because of an existing Marion upstate.

Easton (Washington) Named after the city of Easton, Connecticut, by early settlers from there.

East Marion (Suffolk) named to honor General Francis Marion (Swamp Fox), military leader during the American Revolutionary War. "East" was added because of another Marion in upstate New York.

East Park (Dutchess) Name describes "park" like area located "east" of the Hudson River.

Eaton (Madison) Named to honor General William Eaton, American Revolutionary War leader.

Eddyville (Cattaraugus) Named to honor Thomas Eddy, statesman and "ville" derived from the Latin word "villa" for village.

Eden (Erie) Named after The Garden of "Eden", because of the fertile soil in the area, that made the town prosperous.

Edenville (Orange) Named for it's location near Mount "Eve" and the reference to The Garden of Eden and "ville" derived from the Latin word "villa" for village.

Edinburg (Saratoga) Named after the city of Edinburgh, Scotland, the reason that the "h" was dropped is not known.

Edmeston (Chenango) Named to honor Colonel Edmeston, officer in the French and Indian Wars.

Edmeston (Otsego) Named for Robert Edmeston, early setter.

Edmmons (Otsego) Named for Ebenezer Edmmons, surveyor of the area.

Edwards (Saint Lawrence) Named for Talmadge Edwards, landowner.

Edwardsville (Saint Lawrence) Named to honor Jonathan Edwards, first Postmaster and "ville" derived from the Latin word "villa" for village.

Elba (Genesee) Named after an island in Mediterranean Sea off the coast of Italy.

Elizabethtown (Essex) Named for Elizabeth Gilliland, the wife of William Gilliland, early settler.

Elizaville (Columbia) Named for Elizabeth "Eliza" Hamilton, daughter of Phillip Schuyler, landowner and "ville" derived from the Latin' word "villa" for village.

Ellenburg (Clinton) Named for "Ellen" Murray, daughter of John Murray, landowner and the English word "burg" for town.

Ellenville (Ulster) Named for Ellen Snyder, early settler.

Ellery (Chautauqua) Named to honor William Ellery, statesman.

Ellicott (Chautauqua) Named for Joseph Ellicott, land agent for the Holland Land Company, landowner.

Ellicottville (Cattaraugus) Named for Samuel Ellicott, early settler and "ville" derived from the Latin word "villa" for village.

Ellington (Chautauqua) Named for the founding Ellington family.

Ellisburg (Jefferson) Named for Lyman Ellis, landowner and the English word "burg" for town.

Elma (Erie) Named for a large elm tree located there, using the Latin version of the name.

Elmira (Chemung) Named for Elmira Teall, daughter of an early settler

Elmsford (Westchester) Named for the Elm trees in the area and the near-by stream crossing or "ford."

Elnora (Saratoga) Named for Elnora Hammond, wife of C. Hammond, supervisor of the D&H Railroad, the town's main industry.

Elsmere (Albany) Named for Robert Elsmere, hero in the novel "Elsmere."

Emmons (Otsego) Named to honor Ebenezer Emmons, statesman

Empeyville (Oneida) Named for the founding Empey family and "ville" derived from the Latin word "villa" for village.

Endicott (Broome) Named for Henry Endicott, partner in the Endicott-Johnson Shoe Company, the town's main industry.

Endwell (Broome) Named for a "shoe" manufactured by the Endicott-Johnson Shoe Company.

Ephratah (Fulton) Name is derived from a Hebrew word "Ephrata" meaning "fruitful."

Erieville (Madison) Named after Erie County and "ville" derived from the Latin word "villa" for village.

Erin (Chemung) Name is the Gaelic name for Ireland.

Erwin (Steuben) Named for Arthur Erwin, landowner.

Esopus (Ulster) Named for near-by stream, name is derived from an Indian word meaning "small stream."

Esperence (Schoharie) Name is derived from a French word meaning "hope" chosen by early settlers, concerning their "hope" for the future.

Euclid (Onondaga) Named for the Greek mathematician and Geometer of ancient Alexandria.

Essex (Essex) Named after Essex County, in which the village located.

Etna (Tompkins) Name is a corruption of Mount "Aetna" located in Italy

Evans (Erie) Named for John Evans, land agent for the Holland Land Company, landowner.

Evans Mills (Jefferson) Named for Ethan Evans, mill owner. Mills were the early major industry of the village.

Exeter (Otsego) Named after the city of Exeter, in England.

Fabius (Onondaga) Named for Fabius a Roman statesman.

Fairfield (Herkimer) Named after the city of Fairfield, Connecticut, by early settlers.

Fair Haven (Wayne) Named because it provided a "safe" or "fair haven" for ships.

Fairmount (Onondaga) Name describes location as a "beautiful mountain."

Fairport (Monroe) Name describes a "safe" or "fair" seaport for ships.

Fairview (Dutchess) Name describes the location as having a "fair" or "pleasant view."

Fairville (Wayne) Name describes the Village as a "pleasent" or "fair" place and "ville" derived from the Latin word "villa" for village.

Falconer (Chautauqua) Named for William Falconer, landowner.

Fallsburg (Tompkins) Named for the "waterfall" located there and the English word "burg" for town.

Farmersville Station (Cattaraugus) Name describes farming as the Village's main business and for railroad "station" located there and "ville" derived from the Latin word "villa" for village.

Farmington (Ontario) Named after the city of Farmington, Connecticut, home of early settlers.

Farnham (Erie) Named for Leroy Farnham, landowner.

Faust (Franklin) Named for an ancient magician, of the same name.

Fayetteville (Onondaga) Name is the shorten American version for the name of the Marquis de Lafayette and "ville" derived from the Latin word "villa" for village.

Felts Mills (Jefferson) Named for John Felts, mill owner. Who built the first Mill in the village.

Fenner (Livingston) Named to honor James Fenner, Governor of Rhode Island , home of early settlers.

Fenton (Broome) Named to honor Reuben Fenton, Governor of New York State.

Ferenbaugh (Steuben) Named for the founding Ferenbaugh family.

Fergusonville (Delaware) Named for the founding Ferguson family and "ville" derived from the Latin word "villa" for village.

Ferndale (Sullivan) Named for "fern" plants that grew in abundance in the "dale" an English word for "valley."

Fernwood (Oswego) Name describes "wooded" area which contained an abundance of "fern" bushes.

Feura Bush (Albany) Name is derived from the Dutch phrase "vurlig bos" meaning "fiery wood", which was the result of the sun shining through pine trees in the area making them appear to be on "fire". It was Anglicized to the present name.

Fillmore (Allegany) Named to honor President Millard Fillmore.

Finchville (Orange) Named for the Finch family, early settlers and "ville" derived from the Latin word "villa" for village.

Findley Lake (Chautauqua) Named for the founding Findley family, early settlers on the lake.

Fine (Saint Lawrence) Named for John Fine, landowner

Fire Island Named for the "fires" that glowed at night, that were used to melt down whale blubber, during the Whaling years.

Fishers (Ontario) Named for the founding Fisher family.

Fish House (Fulton) Named for "fishing camp", that built there by Sir William Johnson.

Fishkill (Dutchess) Name is derived from the Dutch term "vis kill" meaning "fish creek".

Fishs Eddy (Delaware) Named for the abundance of "fish" and the currents that caused "eddys" or whirlpools.

Five Mile Run (Cattararugus) Named for a near-by stream, referring to a straight "five mile section" of the stream.

Flackville (Saint Lawrence) Named for founder John Flack and "ville" derived from the Latin word "villa" for village.

Flanders (Suffolk) Named for Flanders region in the Netherlands, by early settlers, because it reminded them of the region..

Flat Creek (Montgomery) Name describes the "flat" area along the "creek".

Fleischman (Dutchess) Named for Charles Flieschman, village benefactor.

Fleming (Cayuga) Named to honor General George Fleming, American Revolutionary War hero.

Flemingville (Tioga) Named to honor General George Fleming, American Revolutionary War hero and "ville" derived from the Latin word "villa" for village.

Floral Park (Nassau) Name describes numerious "flowers" that grew in the "park" like area.

Florence (Oneida) Named after the city of Florence, Italy.

Florida (Orange) Name is derived from the Latin word "floidus" meaning "covered with flowers", name was adopted when the town reorganized on March 12th, anniversary, date of Ponce de Leon's landing in the state of Florida.

Floyd (Oneida) Named to honor William Floyd, statesman.

Flushing (Queens) Name is an Anglicized version of the Dutch town of "Vlissinger", the town had harbored the founding English settlers.

Fluvanna (Chautauqua) Name is a combination of the Latin word "fluvanna" meaning "river" and "Anna" to honor Queen Anne of England.

Folsomdale (Wyoming) Named for the founding Folsom family and the "dale" or "valley" in which the town is located.

Fonda (Montgomery) Named for Down Fonda, early settler.

Forest (Clinton) Name describes wooded or "forest" location.

Forestburg (Sullivan) Name describes wooded or "forest" area and "burg" the English word for town.

Forestport (Oneida) Name describes that it was once, a "lumbering port."

Forestville (Chautauqua) Name describes the location in a "forested" area and "ville" derived from the Latin word "villa" for village.

Forsyth (Cattaraugus) Named to honor John Forsyth, statesman.

Fort Ann (Washington) Named to honor Queen Anne of England, reason the "e" was eliminated in unknown.

Fort Covington (Franklin) Named for General Leonard Covington, Fort Commander.

Fort Edward (Washington) Named to honor Edward, Duke of York, son of King George II of England.

Fort Hunter (Montgomery) Named to honor Robert Hunter, Colonial Governor of New York.

Fort Jackson (Saint Lawrence) Named to honor President Andrew Jackson.

Fort Johnson (Fulton) Named to honor Sir William Johnson, Colonial English patriot and landowner.

Fort Miller (Washington) Named for General Miller, Fort Commander.

Fort Montgomery (Orange) Named to honor General Richard Montgomery, American Revolutionary War hero.

Fort Plain (Montgomery) Name describes location of the "fort" on the open "plain" or flat land of the Mohawk Valley.

Fort Salonga (Suffolk) Named for the British engineer, who built the Fort Slomgo, for the British during the American Revolution. The name was changed to Salonga, by the U.S. Postal Service.

Fort Tilden (Queens) Named to honor Samuel Tilden, English Colonial Governor. of New York.

Fosterdale (Sullivan) Named for Charles Foster, landowner and the English word "dale" for "valley" in which it is located.

Fourth Lake (Warren) Name describes the geographic location of the "lake" as "fourth" or number four in the chain of near-by lakes.

Fowler (Saint Lawrence) Named for Theodocius Fowler, landowner.

Fowlerville (Livingston) Named for Wells Fowler, early settler and "ville" derived from the Latin word "villa" for village.

Frankfort (Herkimer) Named for General Frank, Fort Commander during the French and Indian Wars.

Franklin (Delaware) Named to honor Temple Franklin, statesman.

Franklinton (Schoharie) Named to honor Benjamin Franklin, statesman and "ton" a contraction of town.

Franklinville (Cattaraugus) Named to honor Benjamin Franklin, statesman and "ville" derived from the Latin word "villa" for village.

Fraser (Delaware) Named for the founder Hugh Fraser.

Freedom Plains (Dutchess) Named by quaker settlers as a place where they had "freedom" for their religion and "flat lands" or "plains" in the area.

Fredonia (Chautauqua) Name is a Seudo-Latin word meaning "place of freedom."

Freehold (Greene) Named because it was in a section of land between two land patents and thus a "freehold" not owned by anyone.

Freeman (Steuben) Named for the founder George Freeman.

Freeport (Nassau) Named because during the Colonial days, ship captains used the port to avoid or "free" themselves of British taxes.

Freetown (Cortland) Named for unsettled "free" area, when the town was established.

French Creek (Chautauqua) Named for early French settlers, who lived near the stream or "creek."

French Mills (Albany) Named for Abel French, owned the first "mill" built in the Hamlet.

Frenchwoods (Delaware) Named for French settlers and the forest or "woods" once located there.

Frewsburg (Chautauqua) Named for the founding Frews family and "burg" the English word for town.

Friendship (Allegany) Named by the settlers to indicate that their village was founded in "friendship" and that it was a friendly place.

Friends Point (Warren) Named by early settlers on the "point" of land, for the "Friend's Land Patent "under which it was settled.

Freysbush (Montgomery) Named for Hendrick Frey, landowner and the Dutch word "bush" meaning green area.

Friendship (Allegany) Name describes the basis on which town was settled

Frost Valley (Ulster) Named for the extreme cold winters the early settlers faced

Fruit Valley (Otsego) Name describes the "fruit" farming in the Valley.

Fulton (Oswego) Named to honor the inventor Robert Fulton.

Fultonham (Schoharie) Named to honor the inventor Robert Fulton and the English word "ham" meaning small village.

Fultonville (Montgomery) Named to honor the inventor Robert Fulton, and "ville" derived from the Latin word "villa" for village, added to distinguish it from, the city of Fulton.

Gaines (Orleans) Named to honor General Edmund Gaines, hero of the War of 1812.

Gainesville (Wyoming) Named after Gaines, and "ville" derived from the Latin word "villa" for village, to distinguish it from the former.

Galen (Wayne) Named for Galen, a Greek physician.

Galeville (Onondaga) Named for the founder John Gale and "ville" derived from the Latin word "villa" for village.

Gallatin (Columbia) Named to honor Abraham Gallatin, statesman.

Gallupville (Schoharie) Named for the founder, Samuel Gallup and "ville" derived from the Latin word "villa" for village.

Galway (Saratoga) Named after the town of Galwayshire, Scotland.

Gang Mills (Steuben) Name is a Scottish word meaning "land grant" and the "mills," that were the town's major industry.

Ganesvoort (Washington) Named for the founder Peter Ganesvroort.

Gardiner (Ulster) Named to honor Addison Gardiner, Lieutenant Governor of New York State.

Gardiners Island (Suffolk) Named for Lyon Gardiner, owner of the island.

Gardinertown (Orange) Named for the founding Gardiner family.

Garfield (Rensselaer) Named for James Garfield, early settler.

Garratsville (Otsego) Named for the founding Garrat family and "ville" derived from the Latin word "villa" for village.

Garwoods (Allegany) Named for the founding Garwoods family.

Gasport (Niagara) Named for springs of in the area that emitted flammable "gases" and the near-by water port.

Gates (Monroe) Named to honor General Horatio Gates, American Revolutionary War leader.

Gay Head (Greene) Named after Gay Head, Massachusetts, by early settlers.

Geddes (Onondaga) Named for the founder James Geddes.

Genesee (Wyoming) Name is derived from an Indian word meaning "beautiful valley."

Geneso (Livingston) Name is a variation of "Genesee."

Geneva (Ontario) Named after the city of Geneva, Switzerland.

Genoa (Cayuga) Named after the city of Genoa, Italy, birthplace of the explorer, Christopher Columbus.

Georgetown (Madison) Named for the founder "George" Ellicott.

German (Chenango) Named for the founder Obadish German.

Germantown (Columbia) Named for early German settlers, who founded the town.

Gerry (Chautauqua) Named to honor Elbridge Gerry, statesman.

Getzville (Erie) Named for the founding Getz family and "ville" derived from the Latin word "villa" for village.

Ghent (Columbia) Named after Ghent in the Netherlands (Holland), by early Dutch settlers.

Gibbs Lake (Fulton) Named for Gibbs family, early settlers on the lake.

Gibson (Steuben) Named to honor Hugh Gibson, statesman.

Gibson Landing (Steuben) Named for the founding Gibson family and the "boat landing" located there.

Gifford (Schenectady) Named for the Gifford family, landowners.

Gilbertsville (Otsego) Named for the founder Abijah Gilbert and "ville" derived from the Latin word "villa" for village.

Gilboa (Schoharie) Named for a mountain in Palestine, name means "bubbling fountain."

Gilmantown (Hamilton) Named for John Gilman, early settler.

Glasco (Ulster) Name derived from a "Glasco" glass company that was once the town's main industry.

Glass Lake (Rensselaer) Named for the Rensselaer "Glass" Factory, once the areas largest business.

Glen (Montgomery) Named for Jacob Glen, landowner.

Glenfield (Lewis) Name describes the "fields" in the valley or "glen."

Glenford (Ulster) Name describes the location as "ford" or water crossing in a valley or "glen."

Glenmont (Albany) Name describes it's location in a valley or "glen" near a hill or "mont" a French word meaning"mountain."

Glens Falls (Warren) Named for the founder John Glen and the near-by waterfalls.

Glen Sprey (Sullivan) Named for term "glen" or valley and "sprey" for a Scottish river.

Glenville (Schenectady) Named for Alexander Glen, early settler and "ville" derived from the Latin word "villa" for village.

Glenwood (Erie) Name describes location of "woods" in the valley or "glen."

Gloversville (Fulton) Named for the "glove" industry that was the city's main industry.

Golan (Monroe) Name was derived from letters taken from the names of five pioneer families, that settled the village.

Goldens Bridge (Westchester) Named for Abraham Golden, who was responsible for building bridge in the village.

Gore (Warren) Name is a personal name or it was intended to describe the triangular piece of land or a "gore" on which it is located.

Gorham (Ontario) Named for Nathaniel Gorham, early settler.

Goshen (Orange) Named after a biblical Egyptian city.

Gouverneur (Saint Lawrence) Named for the founder Gouverneur Morris.

Gowanda (Cattaraugus) Name is derived from an Indian word meaning "valley among the hills."

Grafton (Rensselaer) Named after the city of Grafton, Vermont, by early settlers, who came from there.

Grahamsville (Essex) Named to honor Lieutenant John Graham , killed there during the Battle of Chestnut Woods, during the French and Indian Wars.

Grand Gorge (Delaware) Named for the "large valley" at the head water of the Delaware River.

Grand Island (Niagara) Name is derived from the French word "grand" meaning large, properly describing the large "island."

Grangerville (Saratoga) Named for Harvey Granger, early settler.

Granite (Ulster) Named for the granite mined in the area, which was once the major industry.

Grant (Oneida) Named to honor President Ulysses S. Grant, who was also a Civil War hero.

Graniteville (Rockland) Named for the "granite" mined there and "ville" derived from the Latin word "villa" for village.

Grapeville (Greene) Named after a near-by "Grape Creek," which was so named due to abundance of wild grapes that grew in the region and "ville" derived from the Latin word "villa" for village.

Graphite (Warren) Named for "Graphite" mined in the area.

Grass River (Saint Lawrence) Name is derived from French term "la grasse riviere" meaning "the fertile river."

Grassy Point (Rockland) Named for when the area was a "grassy" undeveloped "point" of land.

Gravesend (Kings) Named after a point of sea coast land located in, England.

Gravsville (Herkimer) Named for Latham Gravs, early settler and "ville" derived from the Latin word "villa" for village.

Great Neck (Nassau) Name describes the "necked" or large area of land that extends out into the waters of Long Island Sound.

Great Valley (Chautauqua) Name describes Valley's large size.

Greece (Monroe) Named after the European country of Greece.

Greenburgh (Westchester) Name is derived from the Dutch term "grain town", indicating that the "town" had "grain" mills that milled the grain grown in the area.

Greenbush (Rensselaer) Name is derived from the Dutch word "grunenbush" meaning "green woods", that has been Anglicized to the present spelling .

Greene (Chemung) Named to honor General Nathaniel Greene, American Revolutionary War hero.

Greenfield (Saratoga) Named after the city of Greenfield, New Hampshire, by early settlers.

Greenfield Center (Saratoga) Named after the city of Greenfield, New Hampshire, by early settlers, who came from there and the that it was the commercial "center" of the area.

Greenhurst (Chautauqua) Named for the "green" color of the shrubs or small trees that grew in the area and the German word "hurst" for thicket or grove, indicating that the shrubs or small trees were dense in the area.

Green Island (Albany) Name is derived from the Dutch word "greyen" meaning "pine island," which was Anglicized to it's present name.

Greenlawn (Suffolk) Named by the Long Island Railroad Authority, for the "green lawn" in front of village's railroad depot.

Greenport (Columbia) Named because the terrain appeared "green" when boatmen approached the "port" from the Hudson River.

Greenport (Suffolk) Named after the near-by Greenport Harbor.

Greenville (Greene) Named to honor General Nathaniel Greene, American Revolutionary War hero.

Greenwich (Washington) Named after the city of Greenwich, England, by early settlers.

Greenwood (Steuben) Name describes the "green" fir tree "forest" that was there when the town was founded.

Greenwood Lake (Orange) Name describes the "green" color of the "forest" on the lakeshore.

Greig (Lewis) Named for the founder John Greig.

Greigsville (Livingston) Named for John Greig, early settler and "ville" derived from the Latin word "villa" for village, to distinguish it from Greig.

Griffin (Hamilton) Named for Stephen Griffin, landowner.

Grifton Corners (Delaware) Named for the founding Grifton family and the location at the intersection of two highways.

Groton (Tompkins) Named after the city Groton, Connecticut, home of early settlers, which was named after the founder William Winthope's estate in England.

Groveland (Livingston) Name describes "groves" of trees in the area, when the town was settled.

Guilderland (Albany) Named after Gelderlandin in the Netherlands, Anglicized by English settlers. The name is for the hereditary province of the Van Rensselaer family.

Guilford (Chemung) Named after the city of Guilford, Connecticut, home of early settlers.

Guyanoga (Yates) Named for the Indian Chief Guyanoga.

Hadley (Saratoga) Named after the city of Hadley, Massachusetts, home of early settlers.

Hagaman (Montgomery) Named for the founder Joseph Hagaman.

Hague (Warren) Named after the city of Hague, in the Netherlands.

Hines Falls (Greene) Named for the founder Aaron Haines and the near-by water "falls."

Halcott Center (Greene) Named for Geroge Halicott, early settler and that the town was a "center" of commerce.

Half Hollow Hills (Suffolk) Name describes the area as having "small or half sized valleys."

Halfmoon (Saratoga) Named for the "half moon" shape of the near-by Hudson River.

PLACE NAMES IN NEW YORK 79

Hale Eddy (Delaware) Named for founding Hale family and "eddy" or whirlpools located in the stream.

Halesite (Suffolk) Named to honor Nathan Hale, American patriot executed during the American Revolutionary War, who was believed to have been captured at this "site" by the British.

Hall (Ontario) Named to honor Lyman Hall, statesman

Halletts Cove (Queens) Named for the founding Hallett family and the near-by body of water or "cove."

Hallsville (Montgomery) Named for the founder Robert Hall and "ville" derived from the Latin word "villa" for village.

Halseyville (Tompkins) Named for Nicholl Haley, early settler and "ville" derived from the Latin word "villa" for village.

Hamburg (Erie) Named after the city of Hamburg, Germany, home of early settlers.

Hamden (Delaware) Named after Hampden County, Massachusetts, home of early settlers, ultimately the "p" was eliminated, for some unknown reason.

Hamilton (Madison) Named to honor Alexander Hamilton, statesman.

Hamlet (Chautauqua) Name describes village's small size.

Hamlin (Monroe) Named to honor Vice President Hannibal Hamlin.

Hammond (Saint Lawrence) Named for Abijah Hammond, landowner.

Hammondsport (Steuben) Named for the founder Lazarus Hammond.

Hampton (Orange) Named after the city Hampton Court, in England.

Hampton Bays (Suffolk) Name is a contraction of "Hampton" from Southampton and the near-by "bays."

Hamtonburgh (Orange) Name is a corruption of Wolver "Hampton", England, birthplace of the founder, William Bull and the Scottish word "burgh" for town.

Hancock (Delaware) Named to honor John Hancock, Signer of the Declaration of Independence and a leader during the American Revolution.

Hannacriox (Greene) Named is derived from the Dutch word "hannekraai" meaning "cock-crowing creek", based on a legend, that a "crowing rooster" floated down the creek on a ice flow.

Hannibal (Oswego) Named for the Carthagian General Hannibal, a great leader of the ancient Carthage, an ancient African city state.

Hardenburgh (Ulster) Named for the Great Hardenburgh Patent, which was named after Johnnes Hardenburgh, early Dutch proprietor or landowner

Harmony (Chautauqua) Named for the founder Peter Harmony.

Harkness (Clinton) Named for the founding Harkness family.

Harlem (Kings) Named after Harlem, New York, home of early settlers, which was named after a town in the Netherlands.

Harpersfield (Delaware) Named for John Harper, early settler and the farming "fields" in the area.

Harpursville (Broome) Named for Robert Harpur, landowner and "ville" derived from the Latin word "villa" for town.

Harrietstown (Franklin) Named for Harriet Duane, wife of founder James Duane.

Harriman (Orange) Named for railroad magnate, E. H. Harriman.

Harris (Sullivan) Named for founder Joseph Harris.

Harrisburg (Jefferson) Named for Richard Harrison, landowner and the English word "burg" for town.

Harrisville (Lewis) Named for the founder Fasket Harris and "ville" derived from the Latin word "villa" for village.

Harrison (Franklin) Named for Richard Harrison, landowner.

Harrison (Westchester) Named for the founder John Harrison.

Harrisville (Lewis) Named for the founder Fosket Harris and "ville" derived from the Latin word "villa" for village.

Hartfield (Chautauqua) Named for the founding Hartfield family.

Hartford (Washington) Named after the city of Hartford, Connecticut, home of early settlers.

Hartland (Niagara) Named after the city of Hartland, Vermont.

Hart Lot (Onondaga) Named after the "Hart Lot" Land Grant

Hartsdale (Westchester) Named for John Hart, landowner and the English word "dale" for valley, in which it is located.

Hasbrouck (Sullivan) Named for Hasbrouck family, early settlers.

Hasenclever (Rockland) Named for the founding Hasenclever family.

Haskinville (Steuben) Named for the founding Haskin family and "ville" derived from the Latin word "villa" for village.

Hastings (Oswego) Named for the founding Hastings family.

Hastings on Hudson (Westchester) Named after the city of Hastings, England, the birthplace of founder, William Saunders and it's location on the Hudson River.

Hauppauge (Rensselaer) Name derived from an Indian word meaning "overflowed land" describing a swampy area.

Harvard (Columbia) Named for the founding Harvard family.

Haven (Sullivan) Name describes a place of safety, for ships.

Haverstaw (Rockland) Name derived from a Dutch term meaning "oat straw" referring to the local hay crop.

Haviland (Putnam) Named for the founder William Haviland.

Hawkeye (Clinton) Named for the Indian Chief Hawkeye.

Hawleyton (Broome) Named for Gideon Hawkley, landowner and "ton" the contraction of "town."

Haynersville (Rensselaer) Named for the founder John Hayner and "ville" derived from the Latin word "villa" for village.

Hebron (Washington) Named after ancient city located in Jordan.

Hector (Schuyler) Named for Hector, legendary Trogan Warrior.

Hemlock (Livingston) Named for the "hemlock" fir trees that grew in the area.

Hempstead (Nassau) Named after the town of Hemel-Hempstead, England, birthplace of an early English settler or for the Dutch term "heemstede."

Hemstreet Park (Rensselaer) Named for Charles Hemstreet, landowner and "park" for the park like appearance of the area.

Henderson (Jefferson) Named for William Henderson, landowner.

Henrietta (Monroe) Named to honor Henrietta Laura, Countess of Bath.

Herkimer (Herkimer) Named to honor General Nicholas Herkimer, American Revolutionary Was hero.

Hermon (Saint Lawrence) Named after a mountain in Syria.

Hermitage (Wyoming) Named after the home of President Thomas Jefferson.

Herrings (Jefferson) Named for William and Fred Herring, mill owners, who were the first to build "Mills" in the village.

Heuvelton (Saint Lawrence) Named for the founder Jacob Van Heuvel and "ton" a contraction for "town."

Hewlett (Nassau) Named for the founder George Hewitt

Hibernia (Dutchess) Name is the Latin name for "Ireland."

Hicksville (Nassau) Named for Valintine Hicks, landowner and "ville" derived from the Latin word "villa" for village.

Higginsville (Oneida) Named to honor Frank Higgins, Governor of New York State and "ville" derived from the Latin word "villa" for village.

High Falls (Ulster) Name describes the "high" elevation of the near-by water "falls."

Highland (Ulster) Name is derived from Dutch word "hogeland" meaning "highland."

Highland Lake (Delaware) Name describes "lake's" location on "high ground".

Highland Falls (Orange) Name describes "high" elevation of the village and the near-by "waterfalls."

Highmarket (Lewis) Named after a district of London, England, home of early settlers.

High Mills (Schenectady) Named for the "high" location of the "mills" on the Alplaus Creek.

Highmont (Ulster) Name describes "high" elevation of the mountain using the French word "mont" for mountain.

High View (Sullivan) Name describes "high" location with an unobstructed "view", of the area.

Hillburn (Rockland) Name describes "reddish color" of sunlight on the trees in the area.

Hillcrest (Rockland) Name describes location on the "crest" of the "hill."

Hillsdale (Columbia) Named for the terrain of "hills" and "dales" or valleys.

Hilton (Monroe) Named for Richard Hilton, early settler.

Hinckley (Niagara) Named for the founding Hinckley family.

Hinmansville (Oswego) Named for the founding Hinmans family and "ville" derived from the Latin word "villa" for village.

Hinsdale (Cattaraugus) Named after the city of Hinsdale, New Hampshire, home of early settlers.

Hoag Corners (Rensselaer) Named for Jonathan Hoag, landowner and the near-by highway intersection.

Hobart (Delaware) Named for the founder John Hobart.

Hoffsman (Montgomery) Named for John Hoffman, early settler.

Hogansburg (Franklin) Named for the founder Michael Hogan and the
English word "burg" for town.

Holbrook (Suffolk) Name is derived from the term "old brook", after a local stream or "brook."

Holcomb (Ontario) Named for the founding Holcomb family.

Holcott (Greene) Named for George Holcott, early settler.

Holland (Erie) Named for the Holland Land Company, landowner.

Holland Patent (Oneida) Named after the "Holland Patent" land grant.

Holley (Orleans) Named for the founder Myron Holley.

Hollis (Queens) Named after Hollis, New Hampshire, home of the founder Frederick W. Dunton.

Hollowville (Columbia) Name describes village's location in a "hollow" or valley and "ville" derived from the Latin word "villa" for village.

Holmesville (Otsego) Named for the founding Holme family and "ville" derived from the Latin word "villa" for village.

Homer (Cortland) Named for the Greek poet, Homer

Honeoye (Monroe) Name derived from an Indian word, meaning a finger lying, based on the legend of a snake biting off a finger of a Indian.

Hoosick (Rensselaer) Name is derived from an Indian word "panhoosic", meaning "stony."

Hoosick Falls (Rensselaer) Name is derived from an Indian word "panhoosic" meaning "stony" and the near-by "water falls."

Hopewell Junction (Dutchess) Name denotes the "hopeful" spirit of the town's people and the railroad "junction" located there or for the Hopewell family, landowners.

Hopkinton (Saint Lawrence) Named for Roswell Hopkinton, early settler.

Hoppogue (Suffolk) Name is a corruption of the Indian word "winganhappague" meaning "sweet water."

Horicon (Warren) Named created by James Fenimore Cooper, for Lake George, in the novel "Last of the Mohigans."

Hornby (Steuben) Named for John Hornby , landowner.

Hornell (Steuben) Named for George Hornell, landowner.

Horseheads (Chemung) Named for the "horse skills", found when the first settlers arrived.

Horseshoe (Saint Lawrence) Named for the near-by "horseshoe" shaped lake.

Houghton (Allegany) Named for the founding Houghton family.

Hounsfield (Jefferson) Named for Ezra Hounsfield, landowner.

Houseville (Lewis) Named for the founder Eleazer House and "ville" derived from the Latin word "villa" for village.

Howell (Livingston) Named for Thomas Howell, landowner.

Howes (Broome) Named for the founding Howes family.

Howes Cave (Schoharie) Named for Lester Howe, discoverer of the cave.

Hubbardsville (Madison) Named for the founder Calvin Hubbard and "ville" derived from the Latin word "villa" for village.

Hubbell Corners (Schoharie) Named for the founding Hubbell family and the near-by highway intersection.

Hudson (Columbia) Named after the near-by Hudson River and for the explorer, Henry Hudson.

Hudson Falls (Washington) Named after the near-by "Hudson" River and the near by "water falls."

Hughsonville (Dutchess) Named for the founding Hughson family and "ville" derived from the Latin word "villa" for village.

Huguenot (Orange) Named for the Huguenots, early settlers.

Hume (Allegany) Named for the founding Hume family.

Humphrey (Cattaraugus) Named to honor Charles Humphrey, statesman.

Humphreysville (Columbia) Named for the founding Humphrey family and "ville" derived from the Latin word "villa" for village.

Hunt (Livingston) Named to honor Washington Hunt, statesman.

Hunter (Greene) Named for John Hunter, landowner.

Huntington (Suffolk) Named after Huntington, England.

Hunterland (Schoharie) Named to honor Robert Hunter, Colonial Governor of New York.

Hurds Corners (Dutchess) Named for founding Hurd family and the near-by highway crossroads.

Hurley (Ulster) Named to honor Colonial Governor Francis Lovelace Baron of Hurley.

Hurleyville (Sullivan) Named after "Hurley", with "ville" derived from the Latin word "ville" for village added to distinguish it from "Hurley."

Hyde Park (Dutchess) Named to honor Edward Hyde, Colonial Governor of New York and the "park" like area.

Hyndsville (Schoharie) Named for the founder, Henry Hynds and "ville" derived from the Latin word "villa" for village.

Ilion (Herkimer) Name is derived from the Latin word "Ilium", the name of ancient Troy.

Independence (Allegany) Named because settlers had the freedom to be "independent" in their village.

Indian Lake (Hamilton) Named for a local "Indian" settler Sabael Benedict, who lived on the "lake."

Indian River (Lewis) Named for Indians that lived along the river.

Ionia (Ontario) Named after an ancient Greek city.

Irondquiot (Monroe) Name is derived from an Indian word meaning "place where waves die", referring to a local bay.

Ironville (Essex) Named for the "Iron" that was mined in the area and "ville" derived from the Latin word "villa" for village.

Irvington (Washington) Named to honor the author, Washington Irving.

Ischua (Cattaraugus) Named is derived from an Indian word meaning "floating nettles."

Inwood (Nassau) Name is an English term meaning "in the woods".

Island Park (Nassau) Describes the "park" like appearance of the island.

Islip (Suffolk) Name after Islip a parish, in England.

Italy (Yates) Named after the European nation of Italy.

Italy Hill (Yates) Named to describes village's location on a "hill" and for the Town of Italy, in which it is located.

Interlaken (Seneca) Named after a town in the European country of Switzerland.

Ithaca (Tompkins) Named after an island off the coast of Greece.

Jackson Corners (Columbia) Named for Jackson Wing, landowner and the near-by highway intersection.

Jacksonville (Tompkins) Named to honor President Andrew Jackson and "ville" derived from the Latin word "villa" for village.

Jamaica (Queens) Named for the Indian tribe "jameco", the name means "beaver people."

Jamesport (Suffolk) Named for "James" Tuthill, who established the "port."

Jamestown (Chautauqua) Named for the founder James Prendergast.

Java (Wyoming) Named after an island in the South Pacific.

Jay (Essex) Named for Peter Jay, landowner.

Jeddo (Orleans) Named after an ancient town in Japan.

Jefferson (Schoharie) Named to honor President Thomas Jefferson and Signer of the Declaration of Independence.

Jefferson Valley (Westchester) Named to honor President Thomas Jefferson and "valley" in which it located.

Jeffersonville (Sullivan) Named to honor President Thomas Jefferson and "ville" derived from the Latin word "villa" for village.

Jenksville (Tioga) Named for the founding Jenks family and "ville" derived from the Latin word "villa" for village.

Jericho (Nassau) Named for a biblical city.

Jerusalem (Yates) Named after an ancient city in Israel, which is also the present capital of Israel.

Jewett (Greene) Named to honor Freeborn Jewett, a Supreme Court Judge.

Johnsburg (Warren) Named for John Thurman, landowner and the English word "burg" for town.

Johnsonburg (Wyoming) Named for the founding Johnson family and the English word "burg" for town.

Johnson City (Broome) Named for George Johnson, partner of the Endicott Johnson Shoe Company, the city's main industry.

Johnsonville (Rensselaer) Named for William Johnson, early settler and "ville" derived from the Latin word "villa" for village.

Johnstown (Fulton) Named was derived by using the the middle name of the founder, Sir William "Johns" Johnson and combining it with town.

Jonesville (Saratoga) Named for the founder James Jones and "ville" derived from the Latin word "villa" for village.

Jordan (Onondaga) Named for Ambrose Jordan, landowner.

Jordanville (Herkimer) Named for Ambrose Jordan, landowner and "ville" derived from the Latin word "villa" for village.

Junius (Seneca) Named to honor the author of the "Junius Letters", that attacked King George III, on his unfair treatment of the American Colonists

Katonah (Westchester) Name is an Indian word meaning "great mountain."

Kattskill Bay (Washington) Name is the combination of the Dutch word "kattskill" for the wild mountain lions "cats" in the area and the near-by stream and the "bay" into which it flowed.

Kelloggsville (Cayuga) Named the for the founder Charles Kellogg and "ville" derived from the Latin word "villa" for village.

Keene (Essex) Named after the city of Keene, New Hampshire, home of early settlers.

Keene Valley (Essex) Named after the near-by village of Keene, New York and the "valley" in which it is located.

Keeseville (Clinton) Named for the founder William Keese and "ville" derived from the Latin word "villa" for village.

Kendell (Orange) Named to honor Amos Kendell, statesman.

Kennedy (Chautauqua) Named for the founder Robert Kennedy.

Kenoza lake (Ulster) Name is derived from an Indian word meaning "pickerel", which were abundant, at one time.

Kent (Putnam) Named for the the founding Kent family.

Kenyonville (Orleans) Named for the founding Kenyon family and "ville"derived from the Latin word "villa" for village.

Kerley Corners (Dutchess) Named for the founding Kerley family and the near-by highway crossroads.

Keuka (Steuben) Name is derived from an Indian word meaning "place for landing canoes."

Kiamesha Lake (Sullivan) Name is derived from an Indian word meaning "clear water."

Kiatone (Jefferson) Named after the near by "Kiatone Creek."

Kinderhook (Columbia) Name derived from Dutch term "kinderhoeck" meaning "children's corner", an area where Indian children played.

King Ferry (Cayuga) Named for the founding King family and the "ferry" or boat that ferried people across Cayuga Lake.

Kingsbury (Washington) Named after the "Kingsbury Land Patent", which was so named because it was authorized by an English king and the English word "bury" indicating that the area was wooded or largely forested.

Kingston (Ulster) Name is a contraction of the term "Kings Town."

Kirkland (Oneida) Named for the "Kirkland Land Patent."

Kirklin (Clinton) Named for the founder Martin Kirklin.

Kirkwood (Broome) Named for founder James Kirkwood.

Knapp Creek (Cattaraugus) Named for the founding Knapp family and the near-by stream or "creek."

Knowerville (Albany) Named for Benjamin Knowner, early settler and "ville"derived from the Latin word "villa" for village.

Knox (Albany) Named to honor General Henry Knox, Revolutionary War leader.

Knoxboro (Oneida) Named to honor General Henry Knox, Revolutionary War leader and the English word "boro" for town.

Knoxville (Albany) Named to honor General Henry Knox, Revolutionary War Leader and "ville" derived from the Latin word "villa" or village.

Knoxville (Steuben) Named to honor Chief Justice John Knox and "ville"derived from the Latin word "villa" for village.

Kortright (Delaware) Named to honor Captain Benjamin Kortwright, officer during the French and Indian Wars.

Kreischerville (Dutchess) Named for the founder B. Kreischer and "ville" derived the Latin word "villa" for village.

Kripplebush (Ulster) Name is derived from the Dutch word "kreupelbush" meaning thicket or "underbrush."

Krugville (Ulster) Named for the founding Krug family and "ville" derived from the Latin word "villa" for village.

Krumville (Ulster) Named for the founding Krum family and "ville" derived from the Latin word "villa" for village.

Lackawack (Ulster) Name is an Indian word meaning "at the forks." Referring to the division of the stream into separate branches.

Lackawanna (Erie) Named for the Lackawanna Steel Company the town's largest industry.

La Fargeville (Jefferson) Named for John Lafarge, landowner and "ville" derived from the Latin word "villa" for village.

Lafayette (Onondaga) Named to honor the Marquis de Lafayette, American Revolutionary War hero.

Lafayettesville (Dutchess) Named to honor the Marquis de Lafayette, American Revolutionary War hero and "ville" derived from the Latin word "villa" for village.

La Grange (Dutchess) Named after the home of the Marquis de Lafayette, to honor him for him for his help during the American Revolution.

Lagrangeville (Dutchess) Named after the Marquis de Lafayette's home in France, to honor him for his help during the American Revolution and "ville" derived from the Latin word "villa" for village.

Lairsville (Oneida) Named for the founder Samuel Lair and "ville" derived from the Latin word "villa" for village.

Lake Bluff (Wayne) Name describes location of the "cliff" on the shore of Lake Ontario.

Lake Bonaparte (Hamilton) Named for Joseph Bonaparte, landowner of the near- by lake.

Lake George (Warren) Named for near-by lake of the same name, which was named to honor King George II of England.

Lake Katrine (Ulster) Named for Catharine Whitaker or "Katrine", early settler.

Lake Luzerne (Saratoga) Named after the city of Lucern, Switzerland, which is also on a "lake", reason for the "z" is not known or to honor Chevalier de la Luzerne. The French minister to the United States after the American Revolution.

Lake Minnewaska (Ulster) Name derived from an Indian word meaning "frozen waters."

Lakemont (Yates) Name describes the town's location a "mont" the French word for mountain overlooking Seneca "Lake."

Lake Placid (Essex) Named for the lake's "placid" appearance.

Lake Pleasant (Hamilton) Name describes the "lake" as having "pleasant" appearing waters.

Lake Success (Nassau) Name for "Sucsat" an Indian Chief and the near-by lake.

Lakeport (Onondaga) Name describes "port's" location on Lake Oneida.

Lakeview (Erie) Name describes the town's location, with a "view of the lake."

Lakeville (Livingston) Name describes village's location on Lake Conesus and "ville" derived from the Latin word "villa" for village.

Lakewood (Chautauqua) & (Sullivan) Name describes the"wooded" or forests that once covered the the shore of the "lake."

Lamont (Wyoming) Named for the founding Lamont family.

Lancaster (Erie) Named after the city of Lancaster, Massachusetts, home of early settlers.

Lanesville (Greene) Named for the founding Lane family an "villa" derived from the Latin word "villa" for village.

Langford (Erie) Named for the founding Langford family.

Landsing (Tompkins) Named to honor John Lansing military leader during the American Revolution.

Lansingburg (Rensselaer) Named for Abraham Lansing, landowner and "burg" an English word for town.

Larayville (Jefferson) Named for founder Jacques Leray, reason for change in spelling is unknown and "ville" derived from the Latin word"villa"for village.

Lasalle (Niagara) Named to honor the explorer Robert Civelier, Suer de la Salle.

Lassellsville (Fulton) Named for the founder William Lassell and "ville" derived from the Latin word "villa" for village.

Latham (Albany) Named for William Latham, landowner.

Lattingtown (Nassau) Named for Josiah Latting, early settler.

Laurel (Nassau) Named because the area once had an abundance of laurel trees.

Laurens (Otseto) Named to honor Henry Laurens, statesman.

Lawrence (Nassau) Named Alfred N. Lawrence , landowner.

Lawrenceville (Saint Lawrence) Named for John Lawrence, landowner and "ville" derived from the Latin word "villa" for village.

Lawtons (Cattaraugus) Named for the founding Lawton family.

Lawyersville (Schoharie) Named for Thomas Lawyer, landowner and "ville" derived from the Latin word "villa" for village.

Ledyard (Cayuga) Named for Benjamin Ledyard, landowner.

.Lee (Oneida) Named after the city of Lee, Massachusetts, by early settlers.

Leeds (Greene) Named after the city of Leeds, England.

Leicester (Livingston) Named for Leicester Phelps, landowner.

Leon (Cayuga) Named after the city of Leon, Spain.

LeRay (Jefferson) Named for Leray Chaumont, landowner.

LeRoy (Genese) Named for the founder Herman LeRoy.

Levittown (Nassau) Named for William Levitt, the developer who built the town.

Lewis (Essex) Named to honor Morgan Lewis, a Governor of New York State.

Lewiston (Niagara) Named to honor Morgan Lewis, Governor of New York State.

Lewisboro (Westchester) Named to honor John Lewis, early settler and the English word "boro" for town.

Lexington (Greene) Named after the city of Lexington, Massachusetts, by early settlers.

Liberty (Sullivan) Name was chosen to show the patriotic nature of the town's people.

Lichfield (Herkimer) Named after the city of Lichfield, Connecticut, by early settlers.

Lido Beach (Nassau) Named after the Lido Beach Hotel, which was the first commercial business in the community. The hotel was named after a resort villa in Italy.

Lily Dale (Chautauqua) Name describes abundance of "lilies" that once grew in the valley.

Lima (Ontario) Named after the city of Lima, Peru.

Lime Lake (Cattaraugus) Named because the lake bottom contained fresh water shells, which were processed into "lime."

Limestone (Cattaraugus) Name for the "limestone" terrain in the area.

Lincklean (Chenango) Named for John Lincklean, landowner.

Lincoln (Madison) & (Wayne) Named to honor President Abraham Lincoln.

Lincoln Park (Ulster) Named to honor President Abraham Lincoln and the surrounding "park" like area.

Linden (Genesee) Named for the "linden" forest that once there.

Lindenhurst (Suffolk) Named for the linden trees that lined the main street.

Lindley (Steuben) Named for the founder Eleazer Lindley.

Linlithgo (Columbia) Named after the city of Linlithgow, Scotland, hometown of the founder Robert Livingston, reason the "w" was eliminated is unknown.

Linwood (Livingston) Named after the city of Linwood, Scotland, name is derived from an English word meaning "wood by the lake."

Lisbon (Saint Lawrence) Named after the city of Lisbon, Portugal.

Lisle (Cattaraugus) Named after the city of Lille, France, reason for difference in spelling is unknown.

Litchfield (Herkimer) Named after the city of Litchfield, Connecticut, by early settlers.

Lithgow (Dutchess) Name is derived from the city of Linithgow, Scotland.

Little Britain (Orange) Named after Britain, home of early settlers.

Little Falls (Herkimer) Named for the "little" near-by waterfall, in the Mohawk River.

Little Genesee (Allegany) Named for the near-by"Little Genesee Creek."

Little Valley (Cattaraugus) Name describes the village's location in a small or "little" valley.

Liverpool (Onondaga) Named after the city of Liverpool, England, home of early settlers.

Livingston (Columbia) Named to honor John Livingston, founder of the village.

Livingston Manor (Sullivan) Named for the Livingston Manor, located there.

Livingstonville (Schoharie) Named for the founder Peter Livingston and "ville" derived from the Latin word "villa" for village.

Livonia (Sullivan) Named after the city of Livonia, Estonia.

Lloyd Harbor (Suffolk) Named for founder Joseph Lloyd and the near-by "harbor."

Loch Muller (Essex) Name is the combination of the Scottish word "loch" meaning "lake" and and the founding "Muller" family name.

Locke (Cayuga) Named for John Locke, English statesman.

Lockport (Niagara) Named for nearby "locks" and "port" of the Erie Canal.

Locust Grove (Nassau) Named for the "locust trees" that once grew there in large "groves."

Lodi (Seneca) Named after a town in Italy.

Long Beach (Nassau) Name describes the "long beach" located there.

Long Eddy (Delaware) Named for a "long" section of water that had an "eddy" or whirlpools.

Long Island—Name is derived from the Dutch term "langandt" meaning a Long Island.

Long Lake (Hamilton) Name describes the "lake's long" length.

Loomis (Sullivan) Named to honor Doctor Alfred Loomis, who promoted the area as curative for lung deseases.

Loon Lake (Franklin) Named for the "loon" a fish eating bird, that was once abundant on the "lake."

Lordville (Delaware) Named for Eleazor Lord, President of the Erie Railroad, the town's main industry and "ville" derived from the Latin word "villa" for village.

Louisville (Saint Lawrence) Named to honor the French king Louis XVI and "ville" derived from the Latin word "villa" for village

Loundonville (Albany) Named for the Earl of Loundon, who built a military road through the village and "ville" derived from the Latin word "villa" for village.

Lowville (Lewis) Named for Nicholas Low, landowner and "ville" derived from the Latin word "villa" for village.

Lowman (Chemung) Named for the founding Lowman family.

Lowell (Oneida) Named to honor James Russell Lowell, statesman.

Ludlowville (Oneida) Named after the city of Ludlow, Massachusetts, by early settlers. and "ville" derived from the Latin word "villa" for village.

Lumberland (Sullivan) Name described that this "land", once a major "lumber" market.

Lynbrook (Nassau) Name was created from spelling "Brooklyn" back words, because residents from Brooklyn wanted to keep some remembrance of their old neighborhood.

Lycoming (Oswego) Name is derived from an Indian word meaning "sandy stream."

Lykers (Montgomery) Named for Cornelius Lyker, landowner.

Lyme (Jefferson) Named after "Lyme-Regis", England, shortened through the years for reasons unknown or after the city of Lyme, Connecticut.

Lyons (Wayne) Named for the founder Isaac Lyon.

Lyonsdale (Wayne) Named for Caleb Lyon, early settler and the English word "dale" or valley in which it is located.

Lysander (Onondaga) Named for Lysander, a Spartan General.

Mabbettsville (Dutchess) Named for James Mabbett, early settler and "ville" derived from the Latin word "villa" for village.

Macedon (Wayne) Name derived from Greek word "Makedon" meaning
Macedon Ian inhabitants of ancient Macedonia.

Machias (Cattaraugus) Name is derived from an Indian word meaning "bad little falls."

Mahopac (Putnam) Name is derived from an Indian word "great lake."

Maine (Broome) Named after the state of Maine, by early settlers

Malden Bridge (Columbia) Named to honor J. Malden, the engineer who built the local bridge.

Malden on Hudson (Ulster) Named after the city of Malden, England and the near-by Hudson River.

Mallory (Oswego) Named for the founding Mallory Family.

Mamakating (Sullivan) Named for the Indian Chief Mamakating.

Malone (Franklin) Named for Edward Malone, Irish scholar.

Malta (Saratoga) Named for the "malt" brewery, that was once located there.

Maltaville (Saratoga) Named for the "malt" brewing industry, once located there and "ville" derived from the Latin word "villa" for village.

Malverine (Nassau) Named after the city of Malvern, England. It is not known why the "e" was added to the name.

Mamaroneck (Westchester) Named is derived from an Indian word meaning "place of the rolling stone."

Manchester (Ontario) Named after the city of Manchester, England.

Manhasset (Nassau) Named for the Manhasset Indian tribe. The name means "the island neighborhood."

Manhattan (New York) Named for the Manhattan Indian tribe. the name means "an island and a hill." It is also a Borough of New York City.

Manheim (Herkimer) Named after the city of Manhiem, Germany.

Manlius (Onondaga) Named for a famous Roman General.

Mannsville (Jefferson) Named for the founder H.Mann and "ville" derived from the Latin word "villa" for village.

Manorkill (Greene) Name is the combination of the word "manor" or home and the Dutch word "kill" for the nearby stream.

Maplecrest (Greene) Name describes the abundance of maple trees located on the crest of the hills.

Maplehurst (Cattaraugus) Name describes a "maple" trees and the German word "hurst" for thicket, a dense growth of shrubs that both grew in the area.

Maple Springs (Chautauqua) Name describes "maple" trees and "springs" located there.

Maplewood (Sullivan) Named for the "maple" trees or woods, that grew there when the town was settled.

Marathon (Cortland) Named after the battle, in which the Greeks defeated the Persians.

Marbletown (Ulster) Named for the large amount of "limestone" deposits in the area.

Marcellus (Onondaga) Named for a Roman Pope.

Marcy (Oneida) Named to honor William Marcy, statesman.

Margaretville (Delaware) Named for Margaret Lewis, daughter of Morgan Lewis, landowner and "ville" derived from the Latin word "villa" for village.

Mariaville (Schenectady) Named for "Maria", daughter of founder James Duane, and "ville" derived from the Latin word "villa" for village.

Marilla (Erie) Named for Marilla Rogers, landowner.

Marion (Wayne) Named to honor General Francis Marion (Swamp Fox), military leader during the American Revolutionary War.

Marlboro (Ulster) Named to honor John Churchill, Duke of Marlboro.

Maryland (Schoharie) Named after the state of Maryland, home of early settlers.

Martinsberg (Lewis) Named for founder Walter Martin and "berg" the German word meaning village.

Martinville (Erie) Named for the founder Solomon Martin and "ville" derived from the Latin word "villa" for village.

Masonville (Delaware) Named to honor Reverend John Mason, religious leader and "ville" derived from the Latin word "villa" for village.

Massapequa Park (Nassau) Named for the Massapequa Indian tribe.

Massena (Saint Lawrence) Named for Andre Massena, early settler.

Mastic Beach (Suffolk) Name is a variant of mystic. The reason the name was chosen is not known.

Matinecock (Nassau) Named after Mahtinecock Indians, the name means "hill country."

Matteawan (Suffolk) Name is an Indian word meaning "good fur", which is due to early days, when the area was a peltrie or fur camp.

Mattituck (Suffolk) Name is derived from an Indian word meaning "place without woods."

Mattydale (Onondaga) Named for Francis Matty, statesman and the "dale" or valley in which it is located.

Mayfield (Fulton) Named for the Mayfield Land Patent.

Mayville (Chautauqua) Named for May Busti, daughter of Paul Busti, agent for the Holland Land Company, landowners and "ville" derived from the Latin word "villa" for village.

McDonough (Chemung) Named to honor Commodore McDonough, hero of the War of 1812.

McGraw (Cortland) Named for the founder Samuel McGraw.

McIntyre (Dutchess) Named for Archibald McIntyre, landowner.

McKeever (Hamilton) Named for John McKeever, landowner.

McKnownville (Albany) Named to honor James McKnown, statesman and "ville" derived from the Latin word "villa" for village.

Meads (Ulster) Named for the founding Meads family.

Meads Corners (Putnam) Named for George Mead, early settler and the near-by highway intersection.

Meads Creek (Steuben) Named for the founding Mead family and the near-by creek.

Mechanicville (Saratoga) Named for the workers or "mechanics" of the many local industries and "ville" derived from the Latin word "villa" for village.

Mecklenburg (Schuyler) Named to honor Queen Charlotte Mecklenburg, wife of King George III of England.

Medford (Suffolk) Name is derived from an English place name meaning "the middle ford or crossing."

Medina (Orleans) Named after a city in Saudi Arabia.

Medusa (Albany) Named for the Greek goddess Medusa, so the village would have a very unusual name.

Mellenville (Columbia) Named for founding Mellen family and "ville" derived from the Latin word "villa" for village.

Melrose (Rensselaer) Named after the city of Melrose, Scotland.

Memphis (Onondaga) Named after the city of Memphis, Tennessee, home of early settlers.

Menands (Albany) Named for Loius Menands, landowner.

Mentz (Cayuga) Named after the city of Mentz, Germany, home of early settlers.

Meredith (Delaware) Named for Samuel Meredith, landowner.

Meridian (Cayuga) Name describes a given point on the earth's surface, in this case it was used by surveyors as a place name.

Merrick (Nassau) Named for the "Merickoke"Indian tribe. The name means "barren plain."

Merrill (Clinton) Named for the founding Merrill family.

Messengerville (Cortland) Named for the founding Messenger family and "ville"derived from the Latin word "villa" for village.

Menthol (Delaware) Named because "methyl" alcohol distilling was once the local industry.

Mexico (Oswego) Named after the country of Mexico.

Middleburg (Schoharie) Name describes when the town was the "middle" of three forts located in the valley or after the city of Middleberg, Netherlands, name Anglicized by English settlers the berg was changed during time to reflect the Scottish spelling "burgh."

Middle Falls (Washington) Name describes the town's central location near a water fall.

Middlefield (Otsego) Named after the city of Middlefield, Connecticut, home of early settlers.

Middle Grove (Saratoga) Named for the pine "grove" that separated the eastern and western sections of the village.

Middle Hope (Orange) Name changed from Middletown, because another town had the same name, villagers voted to keep "middle" and add "hope" after a town in Scotland.

Middleport (Orleans) Named for it's location between the villages of Montgomery and Mount Hope.

Middlesex (Yates) Named after the city of Middlesex, Massachusetts, which was named after a county in England.

Milan (Dutchess) Named after the city of Milan, Italy.

Milford (Otsego) Named after the city of Milford, England, home of early settlers.

Millbrook (Dutchess) Named after a local estate of the same name.

Miller Place (Suffolk) Named for Andrew Miller, early settler.

Millerton (Dutchess) Named for Sidney Miller, contractor who built the railroad through the village.

Millport (Chemung) Name describes the town being a milling town and a river port.

Mills (Allegany) Named for Roger Mills, early mill owner.

Millville (Orleans) Named after the milling industry located there and "ville" derived from the Latin word "villa" for village.

Millwood (Westchester) Name describes that the area was known for the milling of lumber.

Milo (Yates) Named for the yellow sirghun called "milo", a type of grass grown in the area, that produced a juice used to make molasses.

Milton (Saratoga) Name is contraction of "mill town", so named for the many mills that were located there.

Milton (Ulster) Named to honor the English poet John Milton.

Minden (Montgomery) Named after a village in Germany.

Mineola (Nassau) Name is derived from an Indian word meaning "palisaded village."

Minerva (Essex) Named for the Roman Goddess of Wisdom.

Mineville (Essex) Named for the mining industry located there and "ville" derived from the Latin word "villa" for village.

Minisink (Orange) Name derived from an Indian word "minsies" meaning main or chief town.

Minoa (Onondaga) Named after an ancient Greek city.

Model City (Niagara) Name describes the "city" as a "model" for other cities to copy.

Modena (Ulster) Named after a city in Italy, birth place of Mary of Modena, wife of James Stuart, Duke of York, later King James II of England.

Mohawk (Herkimer) Name is derived from an Indian word "Caniengas", meaning "people of flint."

Mohegan Lake (Westchester) Named for an Indian , who lived near the lake.

Mohonk Lake (Ulster) Name is derived from an Indian word "moggoneck" meaning" lake in the sky."

Moira (Franklin) Named to honor the Earl of Moira, also a town in Ireland.

Mongaup (Sullivan) Named after a near-by stream, word is an Indian word, meaning unknown.

Monroe (Orange) Named to honor President James Monroe.

Monsey (Rockland) Named for an Indian tribe, also known as the "Muncie."

Montague (Lewis) Named for Montague, daughter of H. Piereport, landowner.

Montauk (Rensselaer) Name is derived from an Indian word meaning "lookout place."

Montebello (Rockland) Name is the Italian word meaning "beautiful mountain."

Montgomery (Greene) Named for Montgomery Stevens, landowner.

Montgomery (Orange) Named to honor General Richard Montgomery, American Revolutionary War hero.

Monterey (Schuyler) Named after the city of Monterey, Mexico.

Monticello (Sullivan) Named after the home of Thomas Jefferson. The name is an Italian word meaning "little hill."

Montour Falls (Schuyler) Named to honor Catherine Montour, Queen of the Iroquois Indians, who ruled the area and the near-by water falls.

Montrose (Genesee) Named for the city of Montrose, Scotland.

Montville (Cayuga) Name describes village's location on a mountain, using the French word "mont" and "ville" derived from the Latin word "villa" for village.

Moody (Franklin) Named for Jacob Moody, landowner.

Mooers (Clinton) Named for Benjamin Mooers, early settler.

Moores Mill (Dutchess) Named for the founder Alfred Moore, early mill owner.

Moravia (Cayuga) Named after a province in the former Austria-Hungary, the name was chosen at a town meeting, because it was good sounding . It is now a part of Czechoslovakia.

Moreua (Saratoga) Named to honor Moreaua, a Marshall of France.

Morehouse (Hamilton) Named for the founder Andrew Morehouse.

Moresville (Delaware) Named for the founding More family and "ville" derived from the Latin word "villa" for village.

Morganville (Genesee) Named for the founding Morgan family and "ville" derived from the Latin word "villa" for village.

Moriah (Essex) Named after a district in Palestine.

Morris (Otsego) Named to honor General Jacob Morris, American Revolutionary War hero.

Morristown (Seneca) Named to honor Gouverneur Morris, landowner.

Morrisville (Madison) Named for the founder Robert Morris and "ville" derived from the Latin word "villa" for village.

Motton (Monroe) Named for the founding Morton family.

Mount Hope (Orange) Name is derived from the Latin word "mons" meaning mountain. and "hope" the expectation of a good future for the town.

Mount Ivy (Rockland) Name describes that the "mountain" using the French word "mount" that once contained an abundance of "ivy."

Mount Kisco (Westchester) Name is derived from an Indian word meaning "wetlands or muddy place."

Mount Morris (Livingston) Named to honor Robert Morris, statesman, using the French term "mount" for mountain.

Mount Vernon (Westchester) Named after the home of President George Washington, who used the French term "mount" for the hillside location.

Mount Willard (Washington) Named for an early settler named Willard and the French word "mount" for mountain.

Mountain Dale (Sullivan) Name describes town's location in a "dale" or valley near a mountain.

Mountain View (Franklin) Name describes town's location with a "view" of the near-by mountains.

Mountainville (Orange) Name describes town's location in the "mountains" and "ville" derived from the Latin word "villa" for village.

Mumford (Monroe) Named for the founder George Mumford.

Munnsville (Madison) Named for A. Munn, early settler and "ville" derived from the Latin word "villa" for village.

Muttontown (Nassau) Named for sheep slaughtered there, for "mutton", once the nation's largest sheep abattoir (slaughtering plant).

Nanticoke (Broome) Named for the Nanticoke Indian tribe. The name means "tide water people."

Nanuet (Rockland) Named for the Indian Chief Nanuet.

Naples (Ontario) Named after the city of Naples, Italy.

Narrowsburg (Sullivan) Name describes village's location in a "narrow" valley and the English word "burg" for village.

Nassau (Rensselaer) Named after a dutchy In Germany, home of early settlers.

Nedrow (Onondaga) Name is the reverse spelling of the founding "Worden" family name.

Nelliston (Fulton) Named for the Nellis Family, early settlers.

Nelsonville (Putnam) Named for the founder, Elisha Nelson and "ville" derived from the Latin word "villa" for village.

Nesconset (Suffolk) Name derived from Indian word "nassiconset", meaning at the crossing.

Neversink (Orange) Name is an Indian word meaning "continual running stream."

Nevis (Columbia) Name is derived from Scottish word meaning "water."

New Albion (Cattaraugus) Name is Latin for "New England."

Newark (Wayne) Named after the city of Newark New Jersey, by early settlers.

New Baltimore (Greene) Reason for the name is uncertain, one version is that surveyors for the land developers were from Baltimore, Maryland, choose the name or sailors on the river thought it looked like Baltimore, Maryland and called it New Baltimore.

New Berlin (Chenango) Named after the city of New Berlin, Vermont, by early settlers.

New Bremen (Greene) Named after the Bremen, Germany, home of early settlers.

Newburgh (Orange) Named after the city of Newburg, Germany, home of early settlers, changed during time to the Scottish "burgh" for town.

New Cassel (Nassau) Named after the town of Cassel, in Germany.

New City (Rockland) Named to designate it as a new residential area or because early settlers considered it a "city" offering a "new" start.

Newcomb (Essex) Named for the Newcomb Family, early settlers.

Newfane (Niagara) Named after the city of Newfane, Vermont, home of early settlers.

Newfield (Tompkins) Name describes "new" land with fields for farming, found by early settlers.

New Hamburg (Dutchess) Named after the city of Hamburg, Germany, home of early settlers.

New Hartford (Oneida) Named after the city of Hartford, Connecticut, home of early settlers.

New Hope (Cayuga) Named by early settlers, for the "new hope" they had in starting the "new" town.

New Kingston (Delaware) Named "New Kingston" after the city of Kingston, New York, home of early settlers.

New Lebanon (Columbia) Named after the city of Lebanon Connecticut, home of early settlers, name is a Semitic word meaning "to be white" probably for white chalk cliffs found in the Lebanon Mountians.

New Paltz (Ulster) Named after "die pfalz" a region in Germany, by early settlers, during time it has been Anglicized to the present name.

Newport (Suffolk) Named after the city of Newport, England.

New Rochelle (Westchester) Named after la Rechelle, France, home of the early French settlers, name Anglicized by later English settlers.

New Russia (Essex) Named for the "Russia" smelting process, used by the local iron industry.

New Scotland (Albany) Named by early Scottish settlers as a "New Scotland" after their homeland.

New Stanford (Delaware) Named after the city of Stanford, Connecticut, home of early settlers.

New Vernon (Orange) Named after the city of Vernon, New Jersey, name is derived from the Latin word "vernus" which relates to spring.

Newtonville (Albany) Named for John Newton, landowner and "ville" derived from the Latin word "villa" for village.

New Windsor (Orange) Named after the city of Windsor, Connecticut, home of early settlers.

Niagara (Niagara) Named for the Niagara Indian tribe. The name means "people of the divided bottom land."

Niagara Falls (Niagara) Named for the Niagara Indian tribe and the near-by waterfalls.

Nichols (Tioga) Named for the founder L. Nichols.

Nicholsville (Saint Lawrence) Named for N. Nichols, landowner and "ville" derived from the Latin word "villa" for village.

Nimminsburg (Broome) Named for the founding Nimmons family and the English word "burg" for town.

Nineveh (Broome) Named after an ancient As Syrian city.

Niobe (Chautauqua) Named for "Niobe", wife of a mythological Greek king.

Niskayuna (Schenectady) Name derived from an Indian word "nistigioone" meaning large cornfields.

Niverville (Columbia) Named for the founding Niver family and "ville" derived from the word Latin word "villa" for village.

Norfolk (Saint Lawrence) Named after the city of Norfolk County, in England.

North Castle (Westerchester) Named after the city of "Castle", Maryland, home of early settlers and for the town's "northerly" location.

North Creek (Warren) Named for it's "northerly" location in the state and the near by "creek."

Northeast (Dutchess) Name describes town's location in Dutchess County.

Northfield (Richmond) Name describes the flat grassy area or "fields" in north end of Staten Island.

Northhampton (Fulton) Named for the "North Hampton Land Patent."

Northport (Suffolk) Name describes location on the north shore of Long Island.

North River (Warren) Named for it's "northerly" location in New York State.

Northumberland (Saratoga) Named to honor George Percy, Earl of Northumberland.

Northville (Fulton) Named because it was the "northern" most point of the district and "ville" derived from the Latin word "villa" for village.

Norton Hill (Greene) Named for the founding Norton family and the near-by hillside.

Norwick (Chenango) Named after the city of Norwick, Connecticut, home of early settlers.

Norwood (Saint Lawrence) Name is the contraction of the term"north woods".

Noyack (Suffolk) Name is from an Indian word meaning "a point or corner of land."

Nunda (Livingston) Name derived from an Indian word "nundoa" meaning "hilly."

Nyack (Rockland) Named for the Nyack Indian tribe, name means "point of land."

Oak Beach (Suffolk) Named for abundance of "oak" trees, that once covered the island and the "beach" resort that once existed there.

Oak Corners (Ontario) Named for a large "oak" tree located at crossroads or "corners."

Oakdale (Suffolk) Named for the "oak" trees that grew in the "dale" or valley where it is located.

Oakfield (Genesee) Name describes the "oak" tree forest and the flat land or "fields" in the area.

Oak Hill (Greene) Name describes the "oak" trees on the "hill", when the town was named.

Oakland (Livingston) Name describes "oak" forest on the "land" when the village was settled.

Oakland Valley (Sullivan) Name describes "oak" forest that once grew in the valley, in which it is located.

Obi (Allegany) Name derived from a Japanese word for "silk sash."

Oceanside (Nassau) Named for it's location on the "ocean shore."

Odessa (Schuyler) Named after the city of Odessa, Russia.

Ogden (Monroe) Named for William Ogden, landowner.

Ogdensburg (Saint Lawrence) Named for Colonel Samuel Ogden, Commander of the fort, built during the French and Indian Wars and the English word "burg" for town.

Ohio (Herkimer) Named after the state of Ohio.

Olive (Ulster) Name is believed to be taken from the Bible, by early settlers to indicate their religious faith.

Old Forge (Herkimer) Named for the "old iron forge" that was once the early main industry of the village.

Olean (Cattaraugus) Named for Olean Shepard, first child born in the village.

Olmsteadville (Warren) Named for the founding Olmstead family and "ville" derived from the Latin word "villa" for village.

Oneida (Oneida) Named for an Indian tribe, name "Oniataaug" means "stone people" or "upright or standing stone."

Oneida Castle (Oneida) Named for the "Oneida" Indian tribe and for a Indian "castle" or "village" that was located there during colonial times.

Oneonta (Otsego) Name is derived from an Indian word meaning "stone place."

Onteora (Ulster) Name is derived from an Indian word meaning "hills of the sky."

Oppenhiem (Fulton) Named after the city of Oppenhiem, Germany, home of early settlers.

Oquaga Lake (Broome) Name is derived from an Indian word meaning "wolf."

Oran (Onondaga) Named after an Algerian seaport city.

Orange Lake (Orange) Named after Orange County and the nearby lake.

Orient (Suffolk) Named to imply that the town was the most easterly of other towns on the North Fork of Long Island.

Oriskany (Oneida) Name is derived from an Indian word meaning "place of the nettles", referring to briars or poison ivy, that was once abundant in the area.

Orwell (Fulton) Named for the founding Orwell family.

Osceola (Lewis) Named for an Indian chief, whose name means "tribal medicine drink."

Ossian (Livingston) Named for a "Ossian" a Gaelic hero.

Ossining (Westchester) Name is derived from an Indian word "ossinee" meaning "place of stones."

Oyster Bay (Nassau) Named for the main industry of the area and the "small bay", on which it is located.

Oswego (Oneida) Name is derived from an Indian word "oshwege" meaning the outpouring, referring to the mouth of the near-by Oswego River.

Oswegatchie (Saint Lawrence) Name is derived from an Indian word meaning "black water."

Otego (Otsego) Name is derived from an Indian word meaning "place of the council rock."

Otisco (Onondaga) Name is derived from an Indian word meaning "water dried" or "shrunken lake."

Otisville (Orange) Named for Isaac Otis, early settler.

Otselic (Chenango) Name is derived from an Indian word meaning "plum creek."

Otter Lake (Herkimer) Named for the large number of "otter", that once occupied the "lake."

Otto (Cattaraugus) Named for Jacob Otto, agent for the Holland Land Company, landowner.

Ouaouaga (Broome) Name is a variant of the Indian word "oouaga" meaning "wolf."

Ovid (Seneca) Named for "Ovid", a Roman poet.

Owasco (Cayuga) Name is derived from an Indian word meaning "lake at the bridge."

Owego (Wayne) Name is derived from an Indian word "the place that widens."

Oxbow (Jefferson) Named for the crescent shaped bend in the near-by river.

Oxford (Chenango) Named after the city of Oxford, England.

Pages Corners (Saratoga) Named for John Page, early settler and the near-by highway intersection.

Painted Post (Steuben) Named for a "painted red post", that was found there, when the town was founded.

Paines Hollow (Herkimer) Named for the founding Paine family and the word "hollow" which means valley.

Palatine (Montgomery) Named for a district in Germany, home of early settlers.

Palatine Bridge (Montgomery) Named for a district in Germany, home of early settlers, and the "bridge" over the near-by Mohawk River.

Palentown (Ulster) Named for Gilbert Palen, early settler.

Palenville (Greene) Named for Jonathan Palen, early settler an "ville" derived from the Latin word "villa" for village.

Palermo (Oswego) Named after the city of Palarmo, Italy.

Palmyra (Wayne) Named for ancient Syrian city, the name "palmyra" means "plam" city.

Pamelia (Jefferson) Named for the wife of General Jacob Brown, hero of the War of 1812 .

Panama (Chautauqua) Named after the country of "Panama" in South America.

Paradox (Essex) Name was chosen by towns people, because it was unusual and made the statement that "life was contradictory."

Paris (Oneida) Named for the founder Isaac Paris.

Parish (Oswego) Named for the founder David Parish.

Parishville (Saint Lawrence) Named for David Parish, landowner and "ville" derived from the Latin word "villa" for village.

Patchin (Erie) Named for the founder Freegift Patchin.

Patchogue (Suffolk) Name derived from an Indian word meaning "turning place".

Patterson (Putnam) Named for the founder Matthew Patterson.

Pattersonville (Schenectady) Named for William Patterson, early settler and "ville" derived from the Latin word "villa" for village.

Pawling (Dutchess) Named for Catherine Pawling, landowner.

Pearl Creek (Wyoming) Named for "white pebbles", that were found in the bottom of the "creek", which resembled "pearls."

Pearl River (Rockland) Named for the nearby stream that contained mussels with "pearls" that were found on the "river" bottom.

Pecksville (Dutchess) Named for the founding Peck family and "ville" derived from the Latin word "villa" for village.

Peconic (Suffolk) Name derived from an Indian word meaning "open field."

Peekskill (Westchester) Named for Jan Peek, early settler and the Dutch word "kill" for near-by stream.

Pekin (Niagara) Named for the founding Perkin family.

Pelham (Westchester) Named for John Pell, landowner and "ham" a contraction of "hamlet", the English word for small village.

Pendleton (Niagara) Named to honor Sylvester "Pendleton" Clark, statesman.

Penfield (Monroe) Named for Daniel Penfield, early settler.

Pennellville (Oswego) Named for the founding Pennell family and "ville" derived from the Latin word "villa" for village.

Penn Yan (Yates) Name was chosen as a compromise between the settlers from Pennsylvania and those from New England, known as Yankees , by using the first syllables of "penn" and "yan" from each name.

Peoria (Wyoming) Named for an Indian tribe, name means "carriers of pack."

Perinton (Monroe) Named for the founder Glover Perinton.

Perry (Wyoming) Named to honor Oliver Hazard Perry, hero of the War of 1812.

Perrys Mill (Clinton) Named for George Perry, mill owner.

Perrysburg (Cattaraugus) Named for founder George Perry and the English word "burg" for village.

Perryville (Madison) Named to honor Oliver Pazard perry, hero of the War of 1812.

Persia (Seneca) Named after the ancient Asian nation of Persia.

Peterboro (Madison) Named for the founder "Peter" Smith and the English word "boro" for town.

Perth (Montgomery) Named after the city of Perth, Scotland, home of early settlers.

Peru (Clinton) Named by French explorers, who referred to the area as the northern "Peru" mountains, hoping to find gold, as was found in the mountains of "Peru" in South America.

Petrolla (Allegany) Name is derived from the word "petroleum" referring to the village's location in the oil region of New York State, change in spelling was to make the name distinctive.

Pharsalia (Chenango) Named for a ancient civil war battle, in which Julius Caesar defeated Pompey the Great.

Phelps (Ontario) Named for the founder Oliver Phelps.

Philadelphia (Jefferson) Named after the city of Philadelphia, Pennsylvania, home of early settlers.

Philipstown (Putnam) Named for Adolph Pilispse, landowner, name Anglicized by English settlers.

Phillipsport (Sullivan) Named to honor "Phillip" Hone, president of the Delaware and Hudson Canal, who was in charge of building the "port."

Philmont (Columbia) Named derived from the name of the founder George "Philip" and the French word "mont" for hill or mountain.

Phoenicia (Ulster) Named after an ancient region of Europe, now the country of Spain and a southern section of France.

Pierrepont (Saint Lawrence) Named for Hezekiah Pierrepont, landowner.

Pifford (Livingston) Named for David Pifford, early settler.

Pike (Wyoming) Named for the founder, Zebulon Pike.

Pinckney (Lewis) Named to honor Charles Pinckney, statesman.

Pine Bush (Orange) Named for the "pine" trees and "bushy" shrub plants that were once abundant in the area.

Pine City (Chemung) Name describes that the "city" was built originally built in a "pine" forest.

Pine Hill (Ulster) Name describes location on a "pine" covered "hill."

Pine Island (Orange) Name describes that the "island" was covered with "pine" trees.

Pine Plains (Dutchess) Name describes that large "plains"or flat lands with "pine" forests once covered the area.

Pine Valley (Chemung) Name describes "pine" trees that once grew in the "valley."

Piseco (Hamilton) Named for the Indian Chief Piseco.

Pitcairn (Saint Lawrence) Named for Joseph Pitcairn, landowner.

Pitcher (Chenango) Named to honor Nathaniel Pitcher, Governor of New York State.

Pittsfield (Otsego) Named after the city of Pittsfield, Massachusetts, home of early settlers.

Pittsford (Monroe) Named to honor William Pitt, English statesman and a near-by water crossing or "ford."

Pittstown (Rensselaer) Named for the founder Peter Pitt.

Plainedge (Nassau) Name refers to the location, on the "edge" of a flat area or "plain."

Plainview (Nassau) Name describes a flat area "plain" or flat land that had an open
"view" of the countryside.

Plainville (Onondaga) Name describes the location of the village on a flat area or "plain" and the word "ville" derived from the Latin word "villa" for village.

Platte Clove (Greene) Name is derived from the Dutch term meaning "flat" and the English word "clove" meaning a canyon or gorge.

Plattekill (Ulster) Name derived from a Dutch word meaning "flat brook" or" claim waters."

Plattsburgh (Clinton) Named for the founder Zephaniah Platt and the Scottish word "burgh" for village.

Pleasant Plains (Columbia) Name describes pretty or "pleasant" flat lands or "plains" where it is located.

Pleasant Valley (Dutchess) & (Steuben) Name describes a beautiful or pleasant valley.

Pleasantville (Westchester) Name describes the "pleasant" or peaceful area, that the settlers found, when the town settled and "ville" derived from the Latin word "villa" for village.

Plessis (Jefferson) Named after a town in France, home of early settlers.

Plutarch (Ulster) Named for Plutarch, the Greek essayist.

Poestenkill (Rensselaer) Named for Jan Barentsen Wemp, landowner, who was known as "poest" and the Dutch word "kill" meaning steam or creek or a Dutch word meaning "foaming creek."

Point Breeze (Erie) Name describes location as a "point" of land where winds provide a regular "breeze."

Point Peninsula (Jefferson) Name is derived from a French term "pointe de la chivelure" meaning crown "point" peninsula.

Poland (Herkimer) Named for the eastern European country, of Poland.

Pomona (Rockland) Named for the Roman goddess of fruits and trees.

Pompey (Madison) Named for the Roman general Pompey the Great.

Port Byron (Seneca) Named to honor the English poet Lord Byron.

Port Chester (Westchester) Named after the city of Chester, England, "port" was added to distinguish it from other towns with the same name.

Port Crane (Broome) Named for J. Crane, the engineer, who was in charge of building the Chehango Canal, which made the town prosperous.

Port Dickinson (Broome) Named to honor Daniel Dickinson, statesman.

Port Ewen (Ulster) Named for John Ewen, president of the Pennsylvania Coal Company, the main early industry of the village.

Port Gibon (Saint Lawrence) Named for the Gibon family, who founded the "port."

Port Henry (Essex) Named for "Henry" Dalliba, the son of James Dalliba, who was responsible for building the "port", which became one the most successful ports on Lake Champlain.

Port Jefferson (Suffolk) Named to honor President Thomas Jefferson, a Signer of the Declaration of Independence and a leader during the American Revolution.

Port Jervis (Orange) Named for John Jervis, principal engineer, who was responsible for constructing the Delaware and Hudson Canal, which became a main "port" in the area, which made the town prosper.

Portland (Chautauqua) Named after the city of Portland, Maine, home of early settlers or the name was drawn out of a hat, to end a debate over a name for the village.

Portlandville (Otsego) Named after the city of Portland, Maine, home of early settlers and "ville" derived from the Latin word "villa" for village.

Port Leyden (Lewis) Named after Leyden a village in the Netherlands , home of early settlers.

Port Washington (Nassau) Named to honor President George Washington, a Signer of the Declaration of Independence and a leader during the American Revolution.

Portageville (Livingston) Named for the access or "portage" across the near-by stream.

Porter (Niagara) Named for the founder Augustus Porter.

Porter Corners (Saratoga) Named for the founder Asahel Porter and the near-by highway intersection.

Porterville (Erie) Named for the founding Porter family and "ville" derived from the Latin word "villa" for village.

Portville (Chautauqua) Named because it was once an important shipping
"port" and"ville" derived from the Latin word"villa" for village.

Potsdam (Saint Lawrence) Named after the city of Potsdam, Germany.

Potter (Yates) Named for the founder Arnold Potter.

Potter Hill (Rensselaer) Named for a man named Potter, who was killed in an accident on the "hill", that occurred during the hamlet's early days.

Potter Hollow (Albany) Named for Samuel Potter, landowner and the "hollow" or valley in which it is located.

Potterville (Warren) Named for Joel Potter, early settler and "ville" derived from the Latin word "villa" for village.

Pound Ridge (Westchester) Named for the "Indian pound" or deer trap once located there.

Poughkeepsie (Dutchess) Named is derived from an Indian word meaning "reed covered lodge by the little water place".

Poughquag (Dutchess) Name is derived from an Indian word meaning "soggy meadow" or a swamp.

Prattsburg (Steuben) Named for the founder Zadoc Pratt and the English word "burg" for village

Pratts Hollow (Madison) Named for John and Matthew Pratt, early settlers and the word "hollow" meaning a small valley.

Prattsville (Greene) Named for the founder Peter Pratt and "ville" derived from the Latin word "villa"for village.

Preble (Cortland) Named to honor Edward Preble, statesman.

Preston Hollow (Albany) Named for the founding Preston family and the valley or "hollow" in which it is located.

Promised Land (Suffolk) Named because the "land" was"promised"for a industry development, but was never accomplished.

Prospect (Oneida) Named for the hopes of the founders of the "prospect", for new lives in their new town.

Protection (Erie) Named because early settlers looked for self "protection", when the town was established.

Providence (Saratoga) Named after the city of Providence, Rhode Island, home of early settlers.

Pulaski (Oswego) Named to honor General Casimir Pulaski, a Polish patriot, who was a hero during the American Revolution.

Pulteney (Steuben) Named for William Pulteney, landowner.

Pulvers Corners (Dutchess) Named for the founding Pulver family.

Putnam Station (Warren) Named for J. Putnam, landowner.

Pyrites (Saint Lawrence) Named for the "Pyrites" mined in the area.

Quaker Street (Schenectady) Named for early "Quaker" settlers and the main "street" of the village.

Quarryville (Greene) Named for mining or "quarrying" in the area and "ville" derived from the Latin word "villa" for village.

Queechy Lake (Columbia) Named after a novel by Susan Warner, who once had a camp on the lake.

Queensbury (Warren) Named after the "Queensbury Land Patent." The name is derived from fact that the Patent was granted by The English Queen Anne and the English word "bury" meaning a place in the woods, which referred to the large forest that existed back then.

Quoque (Suffolk) Name is a corruption of the Indian word meaning "creek flowing through a marsh."

Rainbow Lake (Franklin) Name is derived from an Indian word meaning "rainbow", which occurred seasonally on the lake.

Ramapo (Rockland) Name derived from an an Indian word meaning "blue mountains" or "place of sloping rock."

Randall (Montgomery) Named for Henry Randall, landowner.

Randallville (Madison) Named for the founder Samuel Randall and "ville" derived from the Latin word "villa" for village.

Randolph (Cattaraugus) Named after the city of Randolph, Vermont.

Ransonville (Niagara) Named for Clark Ranson, early settler and "ville" derived from the Latin word "villa" for village.

Raquetta Lake (Hamilton) Name derived from a French word meaning "loud noise", possibly referring to rushing of water during the spring run off or that early explorers left their "raquetts", French for "snowshoes", during the French and Indian Wars.

Rathbone (Steuben) Named for the founder Ranson Rathbone.

Ravena (Albany) Named for the "ravines", that once existed on both sides of the main street.

Raymondville (Saint Lawrence) Named for Benjamin Raymond, landowner and "ville" derived from the Latin word "villa" for village.

Reading (Schuyler) Named after the city of Reading, Pennsylvania, home of early settlers.

Reading Center (Schuyler) Named after "Reading" Township in which it is located and that the village was the "center" of local commerce.

Rector (Schenectady) Named for Zachariah Rector, landowner.

Red Creek (Wayne) Named for the near-by "creek", which was a muddy "red"color.

Redfield (Oswego) Named for Charles Redfield, landowner.

Redford (Clinton) Named for the founding Redford family.

Red Hook (Dutchess) Named for the "hook" shaped land area, covered with "red" berries.

Red House (Cattaraugus) Named for a large "red house" that was once prominent in the town.

Red Jacket (Erie) Named for an Indian chief, who wore a "red jacket", given to him by a English officer, during Colonial times.

Red Oak Mill (Dutchess) Name describes a "mill" that was located near a grove of "red oak" trees.

Red Rock (Columbus) Named for a "red rock" formation, found when the town was settled.

Remsen (Oneida) Named for Henry Remsen, landowner.

Remsenburg (Suffolk) Named for Charles Remsen, a prominent resident.

Rensselaer (Rensselaer) Named for Killian Rensselaer, Dutch patroon , landowner.

Rensselaerville (Albany) Named for Stephen Van Rensselaer, Dutch patroon, and "ville" derived from the Latin word "villa" for village.

Republic (Tompkins) Named to honor our Country, as a Republic of free people.

Resort (Wayne) Name means a place to rest or relax, indicating it as good place for a vacation "resort."

Result (Greene) Name was chosen to show the accomplishment, that the hamlet had been established.

Retsof (Genesee) Name is the reverse spelling the last name of William "Foster." The owner of the salt mine, the main industry of the town.

Rexford (Saratoga) Named for the founder Edward Rexford and "ford" or water crossing, of the near-by Mohawk River.

Rexville (Steuben) Named for the founding Rex family and "ville" derived from the Latin word "villa" for village.

Reynoldsville (Schuyler) Named for the founding Reynolds family and "ville" derived from the Latin word"villa"for village.

Rhinebeck (Dutchess) Name is the Anglicized name for the "Rhein" River and the "Beck" family , who were early settlers.

Rhinecliff (Dutchess) Name is the Anglicized name for the "Rhein" River and the near-by high "cliffs" along the near-by Hudson River.

Riceville (Cattaraugus) Named for founder Oliver Rice and "ville" derived from the Latin word "villa" for village.

Richburg (Allegany) Named for the founder Alvan Rich and "burg" an English word for town.

Richfield (Otsego) Named for the "rich fields" of farm land found in the area.

Richfield Springs (Otsego) Named after the town of "Richfield" and for the "springs" in the area.

Richford (Tioga) Named for Ezekiel Rich, early settler and the near-by "ford" an English word meaning "crossing place on a stream."

Richmond (Richmond) Named to honor the Duke of Richmond.

Richmondville (Schoharie) Named for George Richmond, early settler and "ville" derived from the Latin word "villa" for village.

Richville (Saint Lawrence) Named for Salmon Rich, early settler and "ville" derived from the Latin word "villa" for village.

Rider Mills (Columbia) Named for Jonathan Rider, founder and mill owner.

Ridgeway (Orleans) Named for the pass or passage through the near-by "ridge".

Ridgewood (Cortland) Named for the location of forest or "wood" on the "ridge" or hill.

Rio (Orange) Name is derived from a Spanish word meaning "river."

Ripley (Chautauqua) Named to honor Elazar Ripley, statesman.

Ripanius (Broome) Name is derived from a Latin word meaning "living along the bank of a stream", which describes the town's location.

Riverhead (Suffolk) Named the location at the "head" of navigation on the Peconic River.

Riverside (Broome) Name describes town's location on the bank or "side" of the Susquehanna River.

Riverview (Suffolk) Name describes it's location, with a "view", over looking a "river."

Roanoke (Suffolk) Named after the city of Roanoke, Virginia.

Rochdale (Dutchess) Named after the city of Rochdale, Massachusetts, by early settlers.

Rochester (Monroe) Named for the founder, Nathaniel Rochester.

Rock City (Cattaraugus) Named for "rocky" terrain in which the"city" is located.

Rock City Falls (Saratoga) Name describes the "rocky" terrain, and the water fall located in the village.

Rockdale (Chenango) Name describes the "rocky" location in a "dale" or valley.

Rock Glen (Wyoming) Name describes "rocky" location in a "glen" or a small valley.

Rock Hill (Sullivan) Name describes the location on a "rocky hill."

Rockland (Rockland) Name describes the location in a "rocky land" area.

Rockland Lake (Orange) Name describes "lake's" location in a "rocky" area.

Rock Rift (Delaware) Named for a shallow place or "rift" in the "rocky" terrain.

Rock Stream (Schuyler) Name describes location in a "rocky" terrain and a near-by "stream."

Rock Tavern (Orange) Name describes the "tavern" as being in a "rocky" area.

Rock Valley (Delaware) Name describes location in a "rocky" or stony "valley."

Rockville Centre (Nassau) Named for Reverend Mordicai "Rock" Smith, a religious leader in the districts "centre" or the English version "center" and "ville" derived from the Latin word "villa" for village.

Rockwells Mills (Chemung) Named for the Rockwell family, early mill owners.

Rockwood (Fulton) Name describes the location of a "wooded limestone" area.

Rocky Point (Suffolk) Name describes the location as a large "rocky" mountain or "point" of land.

Rodman (Jefferson) Named for Daniel Rodman, landowner.

Roessleville (Albany) Named for the founding Roessle family and "ville" derived from the Latin word "villa" for village.

Rome (Oneida) Named after the city of Rome, Italy.

Romulus (Seneca) Named for Romulus, a king of ancient Rome.

Ronkonkoma (Suffolk) Name is derived from an Indian word meaning "fishing place".

Roosevelt (Nassau) Named to honor President Theodore Roosevelt

Roosevelt Beach (Nassau) Named to honor President Franklin Roosevelt and the near-by beach area.

Rooseveltown (Saint Lawrence) Named to honor President Franklin Roosevelt.

Rosebloom (Otsego) Name derived from a Dutch word meaning "Rose Tree".

Roslyn (Nassau) Named after the Rosslyn Castle area, in Scotland, the second "s" was dropped with the passage of time.

Rossburg (Allegany) Named for the founding Rossburg family

Rossie (Saint Lawrence) Named for "Rossie" sister of David Parish, landowner.

Rossville (Richmond) Named for the founding Ross family and "ville" derived from the Latin word "villa" for village.

Rotterdam (Schenectady) Named after the city of Rotterdam, Netherlands, by early settlers.

Round Lake (Saratoga) Named for the near-by "round" shaped lake.

Roundout (Ulster) Name is the corruption of the Dutch word "redoubt"referring to a fortification they built there.

Round Top (Greene) Name describes the "round" shape of the mountain near which it is located.

Rouses Point (Clinton) Named for Jacques Rouse, early settler.

Roxbury (Delaware) Named after the city of "Roxbury", Connecticut, by early settlers.

Royalton (Orleans) Named is a contraction of the name "royal town."

Rural Grove (Montgomery) Name describes the area as being "country" in nature or "rural" with a "grove" a small group of trees.

Rush (Monroe) Named for the abundance of "rushes" that grew in the area.

Rushford (Allegany) Named for Benjamin Rush, landowner.

Rushville (Yates) Named to honor Richard Rush, statesman and "ville" derived from the Latin word "villa" for village.

Russell (Saint Lawrence) Named for Russell Atwater, landowner.

Rutland (Jefferson) Named after the city of Rutland, Vermont, home of early settlers, which was named after Rutland County, in England.

Rye (Westchester) Named after the city of Rye, England.

Sabbath Day Point (Warren) Named by The English general Lord Jeffery Amherst , because his army left this "point" of land on "Sunday", the "Sabbath Day."

Sabbattis (Hamilton) Named for the Indian Chief Peter Sabbattis.

Sabael (Hamilton) Named for an Indian named "Sabael", landowner.

Sacandaga Park (Fulton) Name derived from an Indian word meaning "drowned" or swampy land and the "park" area it which it is located.

Sackets Harbor (Jefferson) Named for Augustus Sacket, landowner and the near-by "harbor."

Sagamore Hill (Nassau) Name is an Indian word meaning "chief meeting place."

Sageville (Hamilton) Named for the founder Helekiah Sage and "ville" derived from the Latin word "villa" for village.

Sag Harbor (Suffolk) Name derived from an Indian word meaning "place where stream flows out of lake" and the near-by harbor.

Sailer's Haven (Suffolk) Named as a safe place or "haven" for sailers on Fire Island.

Saint Armand (Essex) Name is believed to be a corruption of Saint Martin.

Saint Bonaventure (Cattaraugus) Named to honor Saint Bonaventure, a teacher or theologian of the Catholic Church.

Saint George (Richmond) Named to honor Saint George, patron saint of England.

Saint Huberts (Essex) Named to honor Saint Hubert, patron saint of hunters.

Saint James (Suffolk) Named after the Saint Jame's Church located in the village.

Saint Johnsville (Montgomery) Named for Saint John's Church, the first church in the village.

Saint Regis (Saint Lawrence) Named to honor Jean Francois Regis, early missionary to the area.

Saint Regis Falls (Franklin) Named to honor Jean Francois Regis, early missionary to the area and the near-by water falls.

Saint Remy (Ulster) Named to honor "Saint Remy" or Saint-Remi, teacher or theologian of the Catholic Church.

Salamanca (Cattaraugus) Named to honor the Duke of Salamanca.

Salem (Washington) Named after the city of Salem, Massachusetts.

Salina (Onondaga) Named for the local salt springs.

Salisbury (Herkimer) Named after the city of Salisbury, Connecticut, home of early settlers

Salt Point (Dutchess) Named for the early settlers custom of making "salt licks" or a "point" to attract deer.

Salt Springville (Montgomery) Named for the "salty springs" located in the village, and "ville" derived from the Latin word "villa" for village.

Sammonsville (Montgomery) Named for the founder J. Sammons and "ville" derived from the Latin word "villa" for village.

Samsonville (Ulster) Named for Henry Samon, early settler and "ville" derived from the Latin word "villa" for village.

Sanborn (Niagara) Named for the founding Sanborn family.

Sands Point (Nassau) Named for John "Sands", early settler and the "point" or the pointed shape of the land projecting into Long Island Sound.

Sandusky (Cattaraugus) Named after the city of Sandusky, Ohio home of early settlers.

Sandy Creek (Oswego) Name describes a stream or "creek", that had a "sandy" bed or bottom.

Sanford (Broome) Named after the city of Sanford, Maine, home of early settlers.

Sangerfield (Oneida) Named for the founder Calvin Sanger and the "fields" or flat lands on which the village was located.

San Remo (Suffolk) Named after "San Remo" a town on the Italian Riviera, by early residents of Italian decent.

Santa Clara (Franklin) Named for the birthplace of the founder John Herd's wife, "Santa Clara", California.

Saranac (Franklin) Name is a word meaning "river that flows through rocks" or "the lake of the fallen stars."

Saratoga Springs (Saratoga) Name is derived from the Indian word "saraghtoga" meaning "place of swift water."

Sardinia (Erie) Named for a hymn of the same name, sung by early settlers.

Saugerties (Ulster) Name is derived from the Dutch term "zager's kietie" meaning Zager's Stream, for an early settler.

Sauouiot (Oneida) Name is an Indian word, the meaning is unknown.

Savannah (Steuben) Name derived from an Indian word "zabana" meaning a level grassy plain.

Savona (Steuben) Named after the city of Savona, Italy.

Saxton (Greene) Named to honor Joseph Saxton, statesman.

Sayre (Chemung) Named for the founding Sayre family.

Sayville (Suffolk) Name is the corruption of the name "Seaville", for it's location on the shore of Long Island and "ville" derived from the Latin word "villa" for village.

Scanton (Erie) Named for the founding Scanton family.

Scarborough (Westchester) Named after the city of Scarborough, England.

Scarsdale (Westchester) Named after the city of Scarsdale, England.

Schaghticoke (Rensselaer) Name is derived from an Indian word meaning "landslide."

Schenectady (Schenectady) Name is derived from an Indian word "schaunactada" meaning "the place beyond the pine plains" or the Dutch term "schoon echten deel" meaning a "beautiful, valuable portion of land."

Schenevus (Otsego) Name is derived from an Indian word meaning "hoeing of corn."

Schodack (Rensselaer) Name is derived from an Indian word, meaning tribal meeting place.

Schoeppel (Oswego) Named for the founding Schoeppel family.

Schoharie (Schoharie) Name is derived from an Indian word meaning "driftwood."

Schroon Lake (Essex) Name is derived from the French term"lac duskaroon" meaning "exquisite lake."

Schultzville (Dutchess) Named for Schultz family, early settlers and "ville" derived from the Latin word "villa" for village.

Schuyler Falls (Clinton) Named for the founding Schuyler family and the near-by water fall.

Schuylerville (Saratoga) Named to honor General Philip Schuyler, American Revolutionary War hero and "ville" derived from the Latin word "villa" for village.

Scio (Allegany) Named after the Greek island of Scio.

Scipio Center (Cayuga) Named for the Roman General "Scipo" and the village which was the local "center" of commerce.

Scipioville (Cayuga) Named for the Roman General "Scipio" and "ville" derived from the Latin word "villa" for village.

Sciota (Clinton) Named for the Greek island of "Scioz".

Scotia (Schenectady) Name is the Latin word for "Scotland", home of early settlers.

Scott (Cortland) Named to honor General Winfield Scott, Civil War hero.

Scottsburg (Livingston) Named for Mathew and William Scott, early settlers and"burg" an English word for town.

Scottsville (Monroe) Named for the founder Isaac Scott an "ville" derived from the Latin word "villa" for village.

Scriba (Oswego) Named for George Sciba, landowner.

Sea Breeze (Monroe) Name describes the location of the village, on the "sea" coast, where" breezes" occur on a daily basis.

Sea Cliff (Nassau) Named because it is on a "cliff" over looking Long Island Sound, which was thought to be part of the "sea" by early residents..

Seaford (Nassau) Named after the city of Seaford, England, home of John Seaman, early landowner.

Seely Creek (Chemung) Named for the founding Seely family and the near-by steam or "creek."

Selden (Suffolk) Named to honor Henry Selden, lieutenant governor of New York State.

Selkirk (Albany) Named for James Selkirk, landowner.

Selkirk Beach (Oswego) Named to honor Thomas Douglas, Earl of Selkirk and the location on the waters edge or "beach."

Sempronius (Cayuga) Named for a famous Roman family.

Seneca Castle (Ontario) Named a "hill" in the area was once a "Seneca" Indians councel camp or "castle."

Seneca Falls (Seneca) Named for the "Seneca Indian tribe and the near-by water "falls." "P EOPLE OF THE STONEY AREA

Sennett (Cayuga) Named for Daniel Sennet, an early settler.

Setauket (Suffolk) Name is an Indian word meaning "land at the mouth of the stream."

Severance (Essex) Named because, it was a new start and a separation or "severance" from the past.

Seward (Schoharie) Named to honor William Seward, Governor of New York State.

Shandaken (Ulster) Name is an Indian word meaning "rapid waters."

Sharon Springs (Schoharie) Named after the city of Sharon, Connecticut and the near-by water "springs."

Shawangunk (Ulster Named for an Indian word meaning "rapid waters."

Shelby (Orleans) Named to honor Isaac Shelby, statesman.

Shelter Island (Suffolk) Name is derived from an Indian word meaning "island sheltered by islands."

Sheperdstown (Jefferson) Named for the founder Thomas Shepherd.

Sherburne (Chenango) Named to honor William Sherburne, English statesman.

Sheridan (Chautauqua) Named to honor Richard Sheridan, English statesman.

Sherman (Chautauqua) Named to honor Roger Sherman, statesman.

Sherrill (Oneida) Named to honor Vice President James Sherrill.

Shinhopple (Delaware) Name is derived from the local residents walking through the "hobble bush" or moosewood bush, brushing their shins (front part of leg from knee to ankle), thus the name "shinhopple", the reason for the change from hobble to hopple is unknown.

Shinnecock Hills (Suffolk) Name is an Indian word meaning "level land."

Shirley (Suffolk) Named for Walter Shirley, early settler.

Sholam (Ulster) Name is a Hebrew word meaning "peace."

Short Tract (Allegany) Name describes the "short tract" or small size of the land grant, on which the town was settled.

Shoreham (Suffolk) Name describes the location of the village on the shore of Long Island Sound.

Shortsville (Ontario) Named for the founding Short family and "ville" derived from the Latin word "villa" for village.

Shrub Oak (Westchester) Named for the abundance of "shrub oaks" that once grew in the area.

Shushan (Washington) Name is derived from a biblical word meaning "palace."

Sidney (Delaware) Named to honor William Sidney, an English admiral.

Siloam (Madison) Named for a sacred water spring, in ancient Israel.

Silver Creek (Chautauqua) Named for the near-by stream or "creek", with a sandy bottom that looked like "silver."

Sinclairville (Chautauqua) Named for the founder Samuel Sinclair and "ville" derived from the Latin word "villa" for village.

Sing Sing (Chemung) Name is derived from an Indian word meaning "little stones."

Skaneateles (Onondaga) Name is derived from an Indian word "skahneghties" meaning a "very long lake."

Slate Hill (Orange) Name describes that "slate" was mined from the area "hills."

Slaterville Springs (Tompkins) Named for the founding Slater family and the near-by water springs and "ville" derived from the Latin word "villa" for village.

Sleepy Hollow (Westchester) Named for "sleepy hollow" or a quiet small valley, referred to in Washington Irving's story "The Legend of Sleep Hollow."

Slingerlands (Albany) Named for the founder Teunis Slingerlands.

Sloansville (Schoharie) Named for the founder Reuben Sloan and "ville" derived from the Latin word "villa" for village.

Sloatsburg (Rockland) Named for the founder Isaac Sloat and "burg" an English word for town.

Smithfield (Dutchess) Named for the founder Peter Smith and an area of "fields" or farming land.

Smiths Mills (Chautauqua) Named for the Smith family, mill owners.

Smithtown (Suffolk) Named for Richard Smith, landowner.

Smithville (Jefferson) Named for the founder Jesse Smith and "ville" derived from the Latin word "villa" for village.

Smyrna (Oswego) Named after a ancient Greek city, it is now the city of Izmir, a Turkish seaport.

Snyders Lake (Rensselaer) Named for Harmon Snyder, early settler on the lake.

Sodom (Warren) Named by early settlers to warn future generations, to avoid evil temptations, that led to the destruction of the biblical city of "Sodom."

Sodus (Ulster) Name is derived from an Indian word "assorodus" meaning "silvery water."

Solon (Cortland) Named for an ancient Greek scholar.

Solsville (Madison) Named for the founding Sols family and "ville" derived from the Latin word "villa" for village.

Solvay (Onondaga) Named for the "Solvay Process" that was used locally in the manufacture of sodium bicarbonate.

Somers (Westchester) Named to honor Captain Richard Somers, hero of the Tripolitan War.

Sonora (Steuben) Named after a state in, Mexico, name means "grand" in Spanish.

Southampton (Suffolk) Named to honor the Earl of Southampton.

Southeast (Putnam) Named for it's easterly geographical location in Putnam County.

Southfields (Orange) Named for the "southerly" location of the "fields" in Orange County.

Southport (Chemung) Name describes the "port's" location "southern" section of the county.

South Valley (Otsego) Name describes the "southern" location of the "valley" in the district.

South Wales (Erie) Named for it's "southernly" location in Erie County and Wales a division of Great Britain on the west coast of England.

Spafford (Onondaga) Named to honor Horatio Gates "Spafford" , author.

Sparkill (Rockland) Name is the Dutch word "spar" meaning fir tree and "kill" meaning stream.

Sparta (Livingston) Named after a city state of ancient Greece.

Speculator (Fulton) Named for the "speculator", who developed the area.

Speigletown (Rensselaer) Name for John Van Derspeigle, early settler, name has been Anglicized to the present name.

Spencer (Tioga) Named for the founder, Jonathan Spencer.

Spencerport (Monroe) Named for Daniel "Spencer", early settler and the near-by "port."

Spencertown (Columbia) Named for the founder John Spencer.

Speonk (Suffolk) Name is an Indian word meaning "to the edge of the stream."

Spier Falls (Warren) Named for William Spier, main investor in the company that built the near by power dam and created the water "falls".

Spit Rock (Erie) Named for a curiously formed "rock" found in the area.

Sprakers (Montgomery) Named for Joseph Spraker, early settler.

Spring Glen (Sullivan) Named for a water "spring" located in the "glen" or valley.

Springport (Cayuga) Named for the many water "spring s" located there and the
"port" on Lake Cayaga.

Spring Valley (Rockland) Named for the water "springs' located in the "valley."

Springville (Erie) Named for the water "springs", located near the village and "ville" derived from the Latin word "villa" for village.

Springwater (Livingston) Named for the"water springs" located in the area.

Sprout brook (Montgomery) Name is derived from the fact that the "brook" was said to "spout" from the Canajoharie Creek.

Staatsburg (Dutchess) Named for the founder Samuel Staats and "burgh" a Scottish word for village.

Stafford (Genesee) Named after the city of Stafford, Connecticut, home of early settlers

Stafford's Bridge (Saratoga} Named for Amos Stafford, builder of the first "bridge" in the village.

Standish (Clinton) Named to honor Miles Standish, one of the Pilgrim leaders, who helped establish the Plymouth Colony, in Massachusetts.

Stamford (Schoharie) Named after the city of Stamford, Connecticut, home of early settlers.

Stanford Heights (Schenectady) Named for the Stanford family, landowner and the high ground or "heights" on which the town is located.

Stanfordville (Dutchess) Named for the founding Stanford family and "ville" derived from the Latin word "villa" for village.

Stannards (Allegany) Named for the founding Stannard family.

Stanwick (Oneida) Named for General John Stanwick builder of a fort, that was once located there.

Stark (Jefferson) Named to honor General John Stark, American Revolutionary War hero.

Starkey (Yates) Named for John Starkey, early settler.

Starkville (Herkimer) Named for the founder Eliphalet Stark and "ville" derived from the Latin word "villa" for village.

Star Lake (Saint Lawrence) Named for "star" shape of the near-by lake

Staten Island (Richmond) Name was chosen by the explorer, Henry Hudson to honor the Dutch governing body, that authorized his explorations.

Stedman (Chautauqua) Named for the founding Stedman family.

Stephens Mills (Steuben) Named for the Stephens family, early"mill" owners.

Stephentown (Rensselaer) Named for Stephen Van Rensselaer, Dutch Patroon landowner.

Sterling (Cayuga) Named to honor William Alexander, Lord "Sterling".

Sterlingburg (Jefferson) Named for the founder James Sterling and the English word "burg" for town.

Stetsonville (Otsego) Named for the founding Stetson family and "ville" derived from the Latin word "villa" for village.

Steubenville (Jefferson) Named to honor Baron Von "Steuben", Prussian general, hero in the American Revolution and "ville" derived from the Latin word "villa"for village.

Stilesville (Broome) Named for the founder Rubin Stiles and "ville" derived from the Latin word "villa" for village.

Stillwater (Saratoga) Named for the calm or "still waters" in the near-by Hudson River.

Stissing (Dutchess) Name is derived from an Indian word meaning "great rock".

Stockbridge (Madison) Named after the city of Stockbridge, Massachusetts, home of early settlers.

Stockholm (Saint Lawrence) Named after the city of Stockholm, Sweden, home of early settlers.

Stockport (Columbia) Named after the city of Stockport, England.

Stockton (Chautauqua) Named to honor Robert Field Stockton, statesman.

Stolp (Schoharie) Name is derived from a Dutch word meaning "shade", possibly referring to the fact that the area was thickly forested and "shady."

Stone Arabia (Montgomery) Name is derived from a Dutch land grant, named "Steene Arabia", which was Anglicized to the present name.

Stone Ridge (Ulster) Name describes the location as a "stone" or a rocky "ridge" or a long rocky hill.

Stony Brook (Suffolk) Name is derived from an Indian word meaning "brook laden with stones" or "stony brook" or stream.

Stony Creek (Warren) Name describes the location as an area covered with "stones" and the near by "creek" or stream.

Stony Hollow (Ulster) Name describes "stone" covered "hollow" or valley.

Stony Point (Rockland) Name describes the location as a "stone" covered hill or elevated "point" of land.

Stormville (Dutchess) Named for the founding Storm family and "ville" derived from the Latin word "villa" for village.

Stottville (Columbia) Named for the founder Jonathan Stott and "ville" derived from the Latin word "villa" for village.

Stow (Chautauqua) Named after the village of Stow, Vermont, home of early settlers.

Stratford (Fulton) Named after the city of Stratford, Connecticut, home of early settlers.

Stuyvesant (Columbia) Named to honor Peter Stuyvesant, Dutch Colonial Governor of New Amsterdam, now located in the New York City area of New York State,

Stykersville (Wyoming) Named for George Styker, early settler and "ville" derived from the Latin word "villa" for village.

Suffern (Rockland) Named for John Suffern, early settler.

Sugar Loaf (Orange) Name describes a near-by hill, which in the winter, when snow covered, looks like a white coated "sugar loaf."

Sugar Town (Cattaragus) Named for maple "sugar" processing once the town's main industry.

Sullivan (Madison) Named to honor General John Sullivan, American Revoluntioary War leader.

Sullivanville (Chemung) Named to honor General John Sullivan and "ville" derived from the Latin word "villa" for village.

Summerville (Orleans) Named to honor the Reverend Peter Sommer, a missionary, the reason for change in spelling is unknown and "ville" derived from the Latin word "villa" for village.

Summit (Schuyler) Name describes village's location on the "summit" or hill top.

Summitville (Sullivan) Named because it was located at the highest point or "summit"of the Delaware and Hudson Canal and "ville" derived from the Latin word "villa" for village.

Sunmont (Franklin) Name describes the effect the "Sun" had in making the near-by, mountain or using the French term "mont", appear to shine.

Surprise (Greene) Named for an unexpected event or "surprise", that occurred when the town was founded.

Swain (Allegany) Named for the founding Swain family.

Swan Lake (Sullivan) Named for the abundance of "swans" once found in this lake area.

Swartwood (Chemung) Named for the founding Swartwood family.

Sweden (Monroe) Named after the European country of Sweden, home of early settlers.

Swormville (Niagara) Named for the founding Sworm family and "ville"derived from the Latin word "villa" for village.

Sylvan Beach (Oneida) Name is derived from a Latin word "sylanus" meaning wooded area.

Syosset (Nassau) Name derived from an Indian word "suwasset", meaning "place in the pines."

Syracuse (Onondaga) Named after the ancient Sicilian city of Syracuse, formerly located on the Italian island of Sicily, because the terrains of both were supposedly similar.

Tabery (Oneida) Named after a town in Sweden, home of early settlers.

Taborton (Rensselaer) Name means "promised land".

Tachkanick (Columbia) Name is an Indian word meaning "there is enough water".

Tahawus (Essex) Name is an Indian word meaning "the cloud splitter", referring to a near-by very high mountain, of the same name.

Talcott (Lewis) Named for the founder Samuel Talcott.

Talcottville (Livingston) Named for Hegekiah Talcott, early settler and "ville" derived from the Latin word "villa" for village.

Talcville (Saint Lawrence) Named for the "talc" mineral mined in the area and "ville" derived from the Latin word "villa" for village.

Tannersville (Greene) Named for the former local tanning leather industry, crediting the "Tanner", who preformed the process of tanning leather hides and "ville" derived from the Latin word "villa" for village.

Tappen (Rockland) Named for the "Tappen" Indian Tribe, name means "people of the cold stream."

Tarrytown (Westchester) There are three theories for the name, one is that it is from the Dutch word "tarwe" meaning wheat, that was grown in the area or for the fact that farmers came to town to"tarry"at the town's taverns or for John Tarry, early settler.

Taylor (Cortland) Named to honor President Zachary Taylor.

The Glen (Warren) Name describes the location in a "glen", which is derived from the Gaelic word "gleann" meaning narrow valley.

Texas (Oswego) Named for the Tijas Indian Tribe, Anglicized to "Texas",which was from the state of Texas, name means "friends or allies".

Three Mile Bay (Herkimer) Named because the "bay is 3 miles" west of the town of Chaumont.

Thendara (Hamilton) Name is an Indian word meaning "rim of the forest."

Theresa (Jefferson) Named for "Theresa", daughter of James Le Ray, landowner.

Thomaston (Bronx) Named to honor General John Thomas, American Revolutionary War hero.

Thompson (Broome) Named for William Thompson, early settler.

Thorson (Washington) Named to honor Matthew Thorson, statesman.

Thornwood (Westchester) Name source is unknown, possibly named for the thorny shrubs or "woods" or for some early settler named "Thorn."

Throopsville (Cayuga) Named to honor Enos Throop, a Governor of New York Sate and "ville" derived from the Latin word "villa" for village.

Thurman (Warren) Named for John Thurman, landowner.

Thurston (Steuben) Named for William Thurston, landowner.

Ticonderoga (Essex) Name derived from an Indian word "chigonderoga" meaning "between lakes."

Tillson (Ulster) Named for George Tillson, early settler.

Tioga Center (Tioga) Named after Tioga County and that the town was "center" of commerce for the area.

Tivoli (Dutchess) Named after an estate , once located in the village.

Tompkinsville (Richmond) Named to honor Daniel Tompkins, Governor of New York State and "ville" derived from the Latin word "villa" for village.

Tonawanda (Erie) Name derived from an Indian word meaning "swift water."

Torrey (Yates) Named for the founder Enry Torrey.

Tottonville (Richmond) Named for the founding Totton family and "ville" derived from the Latin word "villa" for village.

Town Line (Erie) Named for a "line" drawn to separate northern and southern sympathizers in the "town."

Townsend (Schuyler) Named after the city of Townsend, Massachusetts, home of early settlers.

Treadwell (Delaware) Named for Thomas Treadwell, early settler.

Trenton (Oneida) Named after the city of Trenton, New Jersey, home of early settlers., which was named for William Trent, early landowner.

Triangle (Broome) Named for the "triangle" shape of the land grant on which was located.

Tribes Hill (Montgomery) Name describes the "hill" that was the meeting place for local Indian "tribes."

Troupsburg (Seneca) Named for the founder Robert Troup and the English word "burg" for town.

Trout Creek (Delaware) Named for the stream or "creek", that once had an abundance of "trout."

Trout River (Franklin) Named for the abundance of "trout" that once were found in the "river."

Troy (Rensselaer) Named after the ancient city of Troy.

Trudeau (Franklin) Named for the founder Doctor E. Trudeau.

Trumansburg (Seneca) Named for Abner Treman, early settler, reason for change in spelling is unknown, and the English word "burg" for town.

Truxton (Cortland) Named to honor Commodore Truxton, hero in the American Revolutionary War.

Tuckahoe (Westchester) Name is derived from an Indian word "tackahog" name of a tuber type vegetable grown in the area.

Tupper Lake (Franklin) Named for J.Tupper, who was responsible for bringing the railroad to the lakeside village.

Turin (Onondaga) Named after the city of Turin, Italy.

Tusten (Sullivan) Named to honor Colonel Benjamin Tusten, hero of the French and Indian Wars.

Tuxedo Park (Rockland) Name derived from an Indian word meaning "round foot" referring to the wolfs found in the area and the "park" like appearance of the area.

Tyrone (Schuyler) Named for the founding Tyrone family.

Ulsterville (Ulster) Named after Ulster County, in which it is located and "ville" derived from the Latin word "villa" for village.

Unadilla (Otsego) Name derived from an Indian word meaning "meeting place."

Union (Broome) Named for the location, where two units of General Sullivan's Army met in 1779.

Union Springs (Cayuga) Named because several water "springs" joined together or "united" when the town was settled.

Uniondale (Nassau) Named to honor the "union" of the United States of America and the English word "dale" for valley.

Unionville (Albany) Named for the "Union" Church around which the community grew and "ville" derived from the Latin word "villa" for village.

Unionville (Orange) Name was chosen after a land dispute between the town's people, was settled, to show renewed friendship and "ville" derived from the Latin word "villa" for village.

Upper Lake (Tioga) Name describes the lake's northern location in the county.

Urbana (Steuben) Named to indicate the change from the country or "rural" setting to a "urban" or town setting.

Ushers (Saratoga) Named for the founding Usher family.

Utica (Oneida) Named after an ancient city in Africa.

Vail Mills (Fulton) Named for William Vail, early lumber mill owner.

Valatie (Columbia) Name is a Dutch word meaning "little falls" in a valley.

Valhalla (Westchester) Name is derived from Norse mythology, meaning "great hall of dead heroes."

Valley Cottage (Rockland) Named for a "cottage" in the valley owned by Robert Green, landowner.

Valley Falls (Rensselaer) Name describes the water "falls" located in the "valley."

Valley Stream (Nassau) Named for the many "streams" that flowed in the "valley."

Valois (Seneca) Named for a branch of the royal French family.

Van Buren Point (Chautauqua) Named to honor President Martin Van Buren and the "point" of land on which it is located.

Vandeusenville (Montgomery) Named for the founder Jutus Vandeusen and "ville" derived from the Latin word "villa" for village.

Van Etten (Chemung) Named for James Van Etten, landowner.

Van Hornesville (Herkimer) Named for the founder Abraham Van Horne and"ville" derived from the Latin word "villa" for village.

Varysburg (Wyoming) Named for William Vary, early settler and the English word "burg" for town.

Vega (Delaware) Named for the star, Vega.

Verbank (Dutchess) Name is derived from a Dutch word "verdant" meaning the near-by hillsides are "green with vegetation."

Vermontville (Franklin) Named after the state of Vermont and "ville" derived from the Latin word "villa" for village.

Vernon (Oneida) Name is a contraction of Mount "Vernon", home of President George Washington, so named to honor the country's first President.

Verplank (Westchester) Named for the founder, Gulian Verplank,

Versailles (Cattaraugus) Named after the city of Versailles, France.

Vesper (Onondaga) Name is a Latin word meaning "evening star".

Vestal (Broome) Name is derived from the name of the Roman Goddess "Vesta" the goddess of health.

Veteran (Ulster) Named to honor veterans, by the town's residents.

Vichers Ferry (Saratoga) Named for the Vicher family, who started the "ferry" that transported or ferried people across the nearby Mohawk River.

Victor (Ontario) Named for the early settlers being "victors" in a battle during the French and Indian Wars or for Claudius "Victor" Boughton, statesman.

Victory (Cayuga) Named for the"victory" in forcing a separation from the town of Cato, by local townspeople.

Victory Mills (Saratoga) Named for the "Victory" Manufacturing Company, who owned the "mills", which was the town's main industry.

Vienna (Oneida) Named after the city of Vienna, in Austria.

Villenova (Chautauqua) Name is a Spanish word meaning "new town."

Virgil (Cortland) Named for the Roman poet Pulleous Vergillius Maro, known as "Virgil."

Voorheesville (Albany) Named to honor Alonzo Voorhees, statesman and "ville" derived from the Latin word "villa" for village.

Vrooman (Schoharie) Named for Peter Vrooman, landowner.

Waddington (Richmond) Named for Joshua Waddington, landowner.

Wading River (Suffolk) Name is derived from an Indian word meaning "the river where we wade for clams."

GAZD

Wainscott (Suffolk) Name is derived from the method of preparing "Wainscott oaken timber or boarding."

Wadsworth (Livingston) Named for the founder Jeremiah Wadsworth.

Walden (Orange) Named to honor Jacob Walden, landowner.

Wales Center (Erie) Named after the division Wales of Great Britain, located on the western coast of England, an that the town was "center" of local commerce.

Walker (Monroe) Named to honor Robert Walker, statesman.

Walker Valley (Ulster) Named for the founding Walker family and the "valley" in which it is located.

Wallace (Steuben) Named for the founder Alexander Wallace.

Wallington (Wayne) Named for the founding Wallington family.

Wallkill (Ulster) Name is derived from there Dutch word "waalkill", which refers to the Waal River in the Netherlands or "walle" meaning wall and "kill" or stream , walled in by high river banks.

Walton (Delaware) Named for William Walton, landowner.

Walworth (Wayne) Named to honor the scholar Reuben Walworth.

Wampsville (Madison) Named for "Wampus" an Indian Chief, reason for change in spelling is unknown and "ville" derived from the Latin word "villa" for village.

Wanakah (Erie) Name is an Indian word meaning "good land."

Wanakena (Saint Lawrence) Name is an Indian word meaning "pleasant place."

Wantagh (Nassau) Name is derived from the Indian word "Wyandach", name of an Indian chief.

Wappinger Falls (Dutchess) Name is derived from an Indian tribe named "Wappinoes", name means "easterners" and the near-by water "falls."

Warners (Onondaga) Named for the founding Warner family.

Warners Lake (Albany) Named for Johannes and Christopher Warner, early settler on the "lake."

Warnerville (Schoharie) Named for the founder George Warner and"ville" derived from the Latin word "villa" for village.

Warren (Herkimer) Named to honor Joseph Warren, who was killed at the Battle of Bunker Hill, during the American Revolutionary War.

Warrensburg (Warren) Named for James Warren, early settler and the English word "burg" for town.

Warsaw (Wyoming) Named after the city of Warsaw, Poland.

Warwick (Orange) Named after the city of Warwick, England.

Washingtonville (Orange) Named to honor President George Washington and "ville" derived from the Latin word "villa" for village.

Wassaic (Dutchess) Name is an Indian word meaning "rock place".

Waterford (Saratoga) Named for the near-by Colonial fording place across the Mohawk River.

Waterloo (Seneca) Named for a town in the European country of Belgium, where the Duke of Wellington defeated Napoleon's Army.

Watertown (Jefferson) Named after the city of Watertown, Connecticut.

Waterville (Oneida) Named after the city of Waterville, Maine, home of early settlers.

Watervliet (Albany) Name is derived from a Dutch term meaning "flood tide or rolling water", referring to the mud flats that changed with tides, on the Hudson River.

Watkins Glen (Schuyler) Named for Samuel Watkins, early settler.

Watson (Lewis) Named for the founder James Watson.

Watsonville (Schoharie) Named for Charles Watson, early settler and "ville" derived from the Latin word "villa" for village.

Watts Flats (Chautauqua) Named for the founding Watts family and the "flat land" in the area.

Waverly (Tioga) Named after the city of Waverly, Massachusetts, home of early settlers.

Wawarsing (Wayne) Name is an Indian word meaning "where the stream flows."

Wawayanda (Orange) Name is an Indian word meaning "winding stream."

Wawbeek (Franklin) Name is an Indian word meaning "rocky place."

Wayland (Steuben) Named to honor the Reverend Francis Wayland, a religious leader.

Wayne (Yates) Named after Wayne County, home of early settlers.

Webatuck (Dutchess) Name is an Indian word meaning "goose."

Webb (Fulton) Named for Samuel Webb, landowner.

Webster Crossing (Livingston) Named for the founding Webster family and the near-by water "crossing."

Webster (Monroe) Named to honor Daniel Webster, statesman.

Weedsport (Cayuga) Named for Elisha Weed, early settler and the near-by "port."

Wellesey Island (Saint Lawrence) Named to honor Sir Arthur Wellesey, the Duke of Wellington and the island on which it is located.

Wells (Hamilton) Named for Joshua Wells, early settler.

Wellsburg (Chemung) Named for the founding Wells family and the English word "burg" for town.

Wellsville (Allegany) Named for Gariner Wells, early settler and "ville" derived from the Latin word "villa" for village.

Wesley (Cattaraugus) Named to honor John Wesley, religious leader.

Westbrookville (Orange) Named for Dirck Westbrook, early settler and "ville" derived from the Latin word "villa" for village.

Westbury (Nassau) Named after a town in England.

West Camp (Columbia) Name describes "westerly" location in the county and that is was a "camp" for early settlers.

Westerlo (Albany) Named to honor the Reverend Eilardus Westerlo, a local religious leader.

Westfield (Chautauqua) Name describes the town's "westerly" location in a farming or "field" area.

Westkill (Greene) Name is the combination of "western" location and the Dutch word "kill" for the near-by stream.

Westmere (Albany) Name describes it's location as the "western" boundry of the city of Albany, using the Dutch term "mere."

West Park (Ulster) Name describes the "park" like area and location "west" of the Hudson River.

West Point (Orange) Name describes the location of a rocky "point" of land on the "west" shore of the Hudson River.

Westport (Essex) Name describes the town's" location on the "west" shore of Lake Champlain.

West Sand Lake (Rensselaer) Name describes the "westerly" location of the lake in relation to "Sand Lake" and the "sand" from the shoreline, once used in the manufacturing of glass.

Westtown (Orange) Name describes "town's westerly" location in the county.

Westville (Otsego) Named for it's "westerly" location in the old town of Constable and "ville" derived from the Latin word "villa" for village.

Westvale (Onondaga) Name describes "westerly" location in the valley or "vale".

Wetherfield Springs (Wyoming) Named after the city of Wetherfield, Connecticut and local water springs found in the area.

Whallonsburg (Essex) Named for the founding Whallon family and the English word "burg" for town.

Wheatfield (Oswego) Name describes "wheat" as the main crop of this farming area of "fields."

Wheeler (Steuben) Named for Silas Wheeler, early settler.

Wheeler (Wayne) Named for John Wheeler, early settler.

Whippleville (Franklin) Named for the founder William Whipple and "ville" derived from the Latin word "villa" for village.

Whiteboro (Oneida) Named for the founder Hugh White and the English word "boro" for town.

Whitehall (Washington) Named for Colonel White and Major Hall, officers in the American Revolutionary War.

White Plains (Westchester) Named for the forest of "white" balsam trees that once covered this flat land area, which early settlers called" the white plains."

Whites Store (Chemung) Named for the founding White family, who built the first "store" in the village.

White Selfware Springs (Sullivan) Named for the "white colored sulfur" in the local water springs.

Whitestown (Oneida) Named for Hugh White, landowner.

Whitesville (Jefferson) Named for the founder Thomas White and "ville" derived from the Latin word "villa" for village.

Whitney Point (Tioga) Named for the founding Whitney family and the "point" of land on which the town is located.

Willard (Schuyler) Named for the founding Willard family.

Willet (Cortland) Named to honor Marinus Willet, a Mayor of New York City.

Williamson (Wayne) Named for the founder Charles Williamson.

Willeston (Nassau) Named for Samuel Willeston, landowner.

Williamville (Erie) Named for Jonas Williams, early settler and "ville" derived from the Latin word "villa" for village.

Williston Park (Westchester) Named for Samuel Willis, landowner. "Ton" was added for town and "park" was added to describe the park like location.

Willowemoc (Sullivan) Name is an Indian word meaning "bottom land."

Willsboro (Essex) Named for William Gilliland, landowner and the English word "boro" for town.

Wilson (Niagara) Named for the founder Reuben Wilson.

Wilmington (Essex) Named after the city of Wilmington, Delaware.

Wilna (Jefferson) Named after a town in Russia.

Wilseyville (Tioga) Named for the founding Wilsey family and "ville" derived from the Latin word "villa" for village.

Wilton (Saratoga) Named after the city of Wilton, New Hampshire.

Windham (Greene) Named after the city of Windham, Connecticut.

Windsor (Broome) Named after the city of Windsor, England.

Wingdale (Dutchess) Named for the founder Alfred Wing and the English word "dale" for valley, in which it is located.

Winnisook (Ulster) Named for a local Indian, named "Winnisook."

Wiscoy (Allegany) Name is an Indian word meaning "under the river banks."

Wittenberg (Ulster) Named after the city of Wittenberg, Germany.

Wolcott (Wayne) Named to honor Oliver Wolcott, Governor of the state of Connecticut.

Wolcottsville (Niagara) Named to honor Oliver Wolcott, Governor of the state of Connecticut and "ville" derived from the Latin word "villa" for village.

Woodbourne (Sullivan) Name is derived from a Scottish term meaning "the forest located on the banks a near-by stream."

Woodbridge (Ulster) Named for the "wooden bridge" which provided easy access to the village.

Woodbury (Nassau) Named for "Woodbury" clove, a Scottish term meaning "dwelling in the woods."

Woodhull (Steuben) Named to honor General Nathaniel Woodhull, a military leader during the American Revolutionary War.

Woodmere (Nassau) Named after the founder Samuel Wood, the addition of "mere" was made to distinguish it from other communities with same name.

Woodridge (Sullivan) Name describes a forest or "woods"located on a "ridge" or hill.

Woodstock (Ulster) Named after a town in Maine, home of early settlers.

Woodsville (Livingston) Named describes the village's location in a forested area and "ville" derived from the Latin word "villa" for village.

Woodville (Jefferson) Named for the founder Jacob Wood and "ville" derived from the Latin word "villa" for village.

Worth (Jefferson) Named to honor William Worth, military leader during the the War of 1812.

Wright (Washington) Named for Silas Wright, statesman.

Wright Corners (Niagara) Named for the founding Wright family and the near-by highway intersection.

Wurtsboro (Sullivan) Named to honor Mauice and William Wurts, builders of the Delaware and Hudson Canal and the English word "boro" for town.

Wyandach (Suffolk) Named for an Indian Chief named "Wyandash."

Wyckoff (Cayuga) Named for the founding Wyckoff family.

Wynantkill (Rensselaer) Named for "Wynant"Gerritse Van Der Poel, mill owner and the near-by "creek" or stream.

Yagerville (Ulster) Named for the founding Yager Family and "ville" derived from the Latin word "villa" for village.

Yaphank (Suffolk) Name is derived from an Indian word "yamphanke", meaning "riverbank."

Yatesville (Yates) Named after Yates County in which it is located and "ville" derived from the Latin word "villa" for village.

Yonkers (Westchester) Name is from the Dutch word "jonker", the title of Anriaen Van Der Donk, landowner, Anglicized to the present name.

York (Livingston) Named after the city of York, Pennsylvania.

Yorkshire (Cattaraugus) Named after the village of Yorkshire. Vermont.

Yorktown (Westchester) Named after the city of Yorktown, Virginia.

Yorkville (Oneida) Named to honor Charles, the Duke of "York" and "ville" derived from the Latin word "villa" for village.

Youngs (Delaware) Named for the founding Young family.

Youngstown (Niagara) Named for the founder John Young.

Youngsville (Sullivan) Named to honor John Young, Governor of New York State and "ville" derived from the Latin word "villa" for village.

Yulan (Sullivan) Named for a flowering "Yulan" Tree of China, which has large white flowers.